Tenuous

Stan Badgett

Tenuous

Globeflower Press

Aspen, Colorado

ISBN-13: 978-0615654119

Globeflower Press

Printed in the United States of America

THANKS

To God for the unspeakable gift of his Son, Jesus Christ, and for his sustaining grace. To my wife for her patience and kindness. To my many friends and mentors who in varying forms and degrees entered into this project with me.

Look unto the rock whence ye are hewn, and to the hole of the pit whence ye are digged.

ISAIAH 51: 1

TENUOUS

CONTENTS

Portions of *Tenuous* appeared in the following publications:

CHAPTERS

Part of "Dust and Trash" as "Rock Dust" in *Minnetonka Review*, Issue 2, 2008; in *The Best Creative Nonfiction: Volume 3*, 2009, W.W. Norton.

"Senior in High School" in *Bayou Magazine* Issue 52, Fall 2009.

An earlier version of "Elephant Buttress" as "Mountain Man" in *Angels on Earth*, September/October, 1997.

Part of "The Intersection" in *Pilgrimage*, Volume 31, Issue 2, 2006; in *Telling It Real: The Best of Pilgrimage Magazine 2003-2008*.

"Premonition" in *Concho River Review*, Volume XXIII, Number 1, Spring 2009.

POEMS

"On the Scene" in *Riversedge*, Volume 22:1, Spring, 2009.

"Inferno" in *Wisconsin Review*, Volume 43, Issue 1, Fall 2008

ILLUSTRATIONS

Burlington

1951

MY EARLIEST memories are soft and moist to me, like my own breath. They are damp with spring green grasses, the lush grasses of southeastern Kansas.

We lived in a white clapboard house in Burlington with tall elms growing beside it. An old-fashioned garden like Farmer McGregor's flourished next door. I remember a woman in a cotton house dress taking me by the hand and leading me through rows of irises, snap peas, ruffled heads of lettuce and plump cabbages. The earth smelled black and wet. She stooped to uproot a carrot, and out writhed a chartreuse snake. My eyes froze on him as he made for cover.

"It's all right," she said. "He's a garter snake. He eats bugs, and I like having him in my garden."

The year was 1951, and I was four years old. The world felt fresh and dense and mysterious. I wanted to explore. My short legs carried me a block away to an old semi-trailer parked in a lot full of weeds. It was an odd sight, alone there. I stared up at the colossal white structure towering overhead with rust stains seeping from its rivets. No words came to describe it. As I ambled home, my fat hand rippled along wire fences. Some saucy girls across the street scolded, "You shouldn't be out of the yard, little boy."

"I can if I want to," I answered.

"We're bigger than you," they said.

I loved my folks. Papa would strum merry songs on the guitar, such as Turkey in the Straw and Buttons and Bows, and get me dancing a jig. Then he'd tease me by singing Goodnight Irene. Mama sang gospel choruses. Happy Day and Oh, How I Love Jesus. Her voice flowed through my soul like warm, sweet honey.

Papa carried me on his shoulders when he went walking. He wanted me up high where I could see the world. I'd clasp my hands around his forehead, or sometimes around his neck. Once he said, "Don't hold on so tight. You've got my Adam's apple."

"Aw, Dad," I answered, "you don't have an apple in your throat." He was tall and skinny with kinky black hair and a protruding larynx that may as well have been an apple.

He pastored the Foursquare Church. His parishioners were farmers, goodhearted folk who sang old-time gospel choruses with shouts and laughter and rambunctious hand-clapping. Sometimes they paid their tithes with dairy goods and vegetables instead of money.

I slept in the attic under a low-sloped ceiling. On the wall at the end of my bed hung a picture of an angel. Black clouds threatened in the background while she hovered in the foreground, smiling on two children crossing a rickety bridge. They looked like Hummel figurines in their lederhosen. I often gazed at that picture and drank solace from it. As it's turned out, I've needed a guardian angel more than once in my life. It reassured me as a little boy to know that God had an angel looking out for me.

A nightmare came to haunt me. I kept dreaming of a washing machine, its agitator churning while a patchwork quilt was stuffed in. The machine labored back and forth while more and more got pushed into it, the agitator straining to digest it all. This dream impinged itself on my sleep night after night. I'd wake in dry-mouthed horror. What did it mean? I think it signified the overwhelming task of ordering the day's events into a meaningful whole. I needed to name everything, but couldn't. Papa built me a rocking horse. How I loved him for that! He liked to putter around with a hammer and saw. He was crawling around the attic one day, in pursuit of some project, when he missed a rafter and came crashing through the ceiling and landed in the bathroom. He

and Mama had a great laugh over it. There was a man-sized hole in the Celotex over the bathtub, and I thought this was amazing and funny.

Mama would sit with me at the foot of the stairs and read evangelistic stories such as *Barney's Barrel,* the tale of an orphan who lived in a trash can. Barney wandered into a store-front church, where he heard the gospel and gave his heart to Jesus. Later he died, but Jesus had a golden crown waiting for him in heaven. On the stoop of that distant stairway, Mama opened her heart and shared with me from the world of books and from her treasure-house of spiritual experience. Reading has stirred me deeply ever since.

A new baby brother, Brent LeWayne Badgett, joined our family in June. Rains were heavy. The Neosho River overflowed its banks. Water stood a foot deep in downtown Burlington. Farmers vacated the lowlands and waited with their cattle in the surrounding hills.

On the Fourth of July the sun came out. I wandered out to the curb and found a paper cylinder with black diamonds twisting around it and a tattered gray fuse protruding from one end. I knew it contained some kind of power if I could just ignite it. A water heater stood in a recess by the stair. I got down on all fours and thrust my hand toward the blue pilot light. Blam. The world came unhinged in a violent flash as my hand shot out of the hole. Electrified, I ran howling through the house. As I ran, I noticed that my hand was covered by a thick mitten of sparkling foam, and that a warm, tingling sensation had replaced the first jolt of pain. I ran to Mama in the kitchen to show her my hand, but there was no injury. I believe God provided that foam mitten as a miraculous protection.

The rain returned. The Neosho spilled over the main road to Burlington, then the town filled up like an oversized bathtub. From there the floodwaters spread out for miles, cutting off town folks from the outside world. We lived at the top of a hill, but down the street from us a boat rescued two men, one clinging to a tree branch, the other to a second-story rain gutter. Papa hoisted me onto his shoulders and took me down to see the damage. He pointed across Main Street. "Look at the snakes." There were swarms of mud-colored ones writhing in the water.

We came to a crowd standing on a hill at the edge of town. They gazed at a fellow in a pitiful little rowboat, dipping his oars against the maelstrom. He was working his way past the great steel bridge, all but submerged, that normally ushered the way into Burlington. "Ladies and gents," announced a man through a megaphone, "let's give a round of applause to the daring fellow who is risking his life to row for help." The crowd cheered and clapped as the boat shrank to a speck on the swirling, shimmering water. One muggy evening after the flood subsided, we went to a house down the street to watch a Rocky Marciano boxing match. A cloud of tobacco smoke hung in the air. A dozen neighbors were crowded into the dark living room, intent on the tiny TV screen flickering in the corner. I remember their dusky forms and laconic voices. Marciano won that fight and all subsequent ones for five years.

That summer I sang my first and last solo at church. Standing proudly next to the pulpit, I peered over the balustrade at a sea of friendly faces and warbled, "Jesus wants me for a sunbeam to shine for him each day." Something tickled their funny bones, and they started chuckling. I was baffled; this was a serious song. Returning to my seat in a flush of embarrassment, I resolved not to sing in public again. I couldn't understand the indulgent way adults sometimes laugh at children.

A month after the flood, nature struck again. We were asleep in our beds when insistent winds began to clatter elm branches against the house. Roused from sleep, I lay in the attic listening to the dissonant moan of the wind. Hailstones peppered the roof. I sat upright as the clatter intensified to frantic clawing. The wind shrieked. Objects in the black of night slammed against the house. Some hellish force was bent on destroying us.

I bolted from bed and clambered down the stairwell. As the storm roared toward the house, I ran for Mama, my ark of safety, her rocking chair somehow silhouetted in the dark living room, and stopped short. Baby brother already occupied the safety of her warm lap. As I stood there frozen in my shoes, it hit me full force that I was on my own— my first acquaintance with a terrible feeling of isolation I would know more acutely in passing years. It was dark, and that's all I can remember about that night.

I wandered in a strangely peaceful world of soft wet grass the next morning while Papa inspected the damage. A large tree lay on the ground next to the house. The wind had ripped it from its trunk and hurled it at the house—but missed. Awestruck, I examined the freshly splintered trunk with its honey-colored shards jutting up in an unruly tangle. The grass glowed all around with emerald softness.

Mama asked Papa what damage had been done, and he told her the garage was gone, and that was it. As a child I envisioned the garage being carried off by the wind, but now I think a tree probably smashed it. Burlington's *Daily Republican* featured the "tornadic storm" on the front page and mentioned the near-miss at the home of Rev. and Mrs. Badgett.

A few days later, this article appeared in the *Daily Republican:*

> *Rev. Russell S. Badgett has resigned as pastor of the Burlington Foursquare church and will go to Durango, Colo., to become pastor of the Foursquare church there. No successor to Rev. Mr. Badgett has been announced.*
>
> *Rev. Mr. Badgett will preach his farewell sermon next Sunday morning, and he and his wife and the children, Stanley Kent and Brent Wayne will leave on the following Tuesday.*
>
> *Durango is a city of about 8,000 population in the southwest corner of Colorado close to Mesa Verde Park.*

BURLINGTON

Rev. Mr. Badgett asks The Daily Republican to express to the people of the church and community his sincere appreciation of the courtesies, kindnesses and cooperation extended him and his family. He says he and his family like Burlington and her people very much and have enjoyed their stay here.

So ended my early days in Kansas. Burlington still clings like a green chrysalis to some velvety leaf in the back of my mind. Inside that chrysalis, bright trees droop like pompons over white frame houses. Mama reads Bible stories to me in warm shadows at the foot of the stairs. Papa hoists me onto his shoulders and strides down a hedge-lined sidewalk. I'm holding tight to his Adam's apple.

Durango

1952-54

THE BOY peeking through the curtain is Stanny-man. His hopeful smile and freckles make him look like Howdy Doody. He watches his father rocking back and forth in front of the red velveteen curtain, heel-to-toe, energized by the gospel message he preaches to the crowded house, warmly exhorting his parishioners to trust in the goodness of God. Someone in the back raises a hand and shouts 'Amen.' Reverend Badgett's congregation loves old-fashioned preaching—the Full Gospel—complete with miracles, healings, and speaking in tongues; shouts, clapping, laughter, and tears. Songs about heaven and Jesus the soon-coming King heartily sung in western-style harmony.

These bright-faced folks meet in a white-stucco building with a crenellated watchtower—the Foursquare church in downtown Durango. Over the curtain stretches a long banner in Old English blackletter: "Jesus Christ the same yesterday, and today, and forever." Stanny asks his mom, "What if somebody doesn't believe what it says?" He's worried someone will be offended.

She answers, "That's why we have it up there. So they'll read it and change their mind."

My family lived in the little parsonage tacked on the back of the rough-stucco church. Though it was cramped, we were happy enough. I slept in a sort of closet. Once, in the middle of the night, God drew me out of bed into the sanctuary, which was dark and empty. Alone there on that stage where my father often stood to preach, I felt the power of God come over me. There were no words of instruction or admonition, just an overwhelming sense of God's presence. It was electrifying, direct, intimate, at once terrifying and reassuring. I spent the next fifty years of my life wondering what it meant.

Grandma Etta Badgett came to visit from California. She had sent me a handmade card when I was small, on which she had pasted a full-length picture of herself in a roomy polka-dot dress, and written, "To Stanley. He is a good boy. Love, Grammo." I miss her. On that visit she lay in bed with me while the evening service gathered momentum in the sanctuary. We could hear the congregation clapping and carrying on out there, but one voice penetrated the air, louder than all the rest. "Whose is that?" Grandma asked with a twinkle. I knew full well it was Mom's.

Dad was an imaginative and visionary man, loaded with quips, low-brow jokes, hayseed colloquialisms, folk tunes from the Depression era, and bright ideas for the ministry. He had landed in Colorado by spinning a globe with his eyes closed and pointing to the first place it stopped. That's how we ended up in this cow town with drunk Indians and shootouts. Dad made side money driving ambulance for the rodeo, hauling bronc busters and bull riders to the hospital. He also transported cadavers across state lines for extra cash. One of his bright ideas: taking Mom out to the West Coast to record gospel songs. He had a pretty decent tenor voice as far as hillbilly voices go. I say "hillbilly," even though he was raised in Los Angeles. After his father died, he moved with his mother to Oregon where he supported her by picking fruit while still a young teenager. They lived in a tent. "This is man's work," an orchard foreman told him. "I can work as hard as any man," was Dad's stalwart reply.

He picked up Okie ways in the migrant camps—spinning yarns with a crooked, sardonic smile; the yodel, the drawl; the brush-a-brush style of strumming the guitar. He and Mom harmonized well. We'd travel up to Silverton, an almost ghost town high in the San Juans, to jam with Keith and Lelia, a pastor couple with an 8-month-old baby. They were pioneering a Foursquare church up there in that bleak mining town—what was left of it. Keith flailed that pedal steel guitar with his glimmering silver bar, and unbelievably exotic tones came sliding out of it like spiced honey. Things heated up; the old floor boards creaked. The four of them took off straight for heaven while the little kid crawled around in his diapers.

When my parents got to the West Coast, Mom heard her own recorded voice for the first time and hated it. She said, "That's it. I'll never do this again." So that was the end of their musical career. But she's been a full-hearted, God-praising woman all her life. The other day on the phone—she's now in her mid-80s—she sang, "He's Got the Whole World in His Hands," just for me.

Another one of Dad's amazing ideas: he rigged the white stucco watchtower on the corner of the church with a drawbridge and lowered it each day for the start of Vacation Bible School, accompanied by a trumpet blast. This may have stemmed from his reading of Dumas' *The Man in the Iron Mask*, which eventually led to a fanciful vision involving him and the Silverton couple, Keith and Lelia, traveling the country as musical evangelists under the banner of "The Three Musketeers."

◆

His father, Harry, had also been a tent revivalist with roots in the Azusa Street Revival of the early 1900s. As a boy, Dad would go out in the backyard and preach to the birds in the treetops; then he'd get out his B-B gun and take shots at them. He conducted his own baptismal service in the backyard, with baby chickens for converts. When Etta came out on the back porch, the drowned chicks were laid neatly in a row. Before she could scold him, he cautioned, "Shhh! They're under the power."

While driving around the streets of LA, Etta got in Dutch with a police officer for a traffic violation. He told her, "You could go to jail for this." While she was trying to smooth things over with the law, Russ looked up at the policeman and said, "You're going to hell, mister."

"You'd better teach that boy some manners," huffed the cop. But

Dad meant it sincerely. This was the kind of preaching he'd heard at evangelistic meetings.

Another time, while on a road trip with his parents, Dad looked out the rear window and exclaimed, "The devil is following us." His mom said, "You're being too imaginative. Don't talk like that." The next thing you know, the back tire went flat.

There was a man running around the countryside named Kenneth Goff who had operated inside the Communist Party, gotten disenchanted, and started working to expose it. Somehow he landed at my dad's church in Durango, where he convened a high-energy meeting unveiling Communist plans to unravel the fabric of America. Those were anticommunist days, unlike the times we live in now. While he was speaking, someone from our congregation saw a mysterious figure hiding behind the curtain. Perhaps a spy or assassin? After that, Dad wanted to buy a gun, but Mom would have none of this. She put the kibosh on it.

◆

The essence of Goff's teaching centered on the idea that the Soviets were subverting America through mass brainwashing—and appealed to patriotic Americans to resist. Was he right? Did we really face such a danger? I think so. There seems to have been no lack of zeal or cunning on the part of Communists to overturn our country from within. My readings over the years have not lessened this impression. Anyway, I was just a kid.

My parents often "hashed out" the issues of the day: the fate of Christian missionaries in China (some of whom Mom had known personally); Truman's refusal to heed Madame Chiang Kai-Shek's pleas for assistance; the brutal treatment of American POWs in Korea; the traitorous Rosenbergs selling nuclear secrets to the Soviet Union. The air was dense with politics. Eastern European countries were falling like dominoes.

◆

In early 1952, my parents hosted a caucus meeting right there on the Foursquare church stage, which I attended, not yet 5 years old. The folks at our get-together voted to draft Eisenhower (who had been somewhat demur) for the presidential nomination. Thereafter, I proudly wore an "I Like Ike" T-shirt until a big kid threatened to thrash me.

The boy peeking through the curtain wants to be a clown. To cavort in baggy clothes, paint an exaggerated frown on his smiley face. Do somersaults. Be part of The Greatest Show On Earth. The neighbor kids parade up the sidewalk—capes, tights, a baton, and a red wagon—to a front lawn where they perform amazing feats under their imaginary Big Top. A ballerina twirls gracefully in her pink tutu; an acrobat hangs by his knees from the weeping willow tree; a fearless

animal trainer in long-sleeve shirt and leather gloves braves an attack
by his pet German shepherd who leaps up and bites his arm. Stanny-
man rolls and tumbles around, ho-ho hee-hee.

Dad had a handful of gags he used over and over: the one where
a hand reached around the corner and grabbed him by the neck—like
a hook jerking him offstage; and the ridiculous business of hugging
himself as if he were in a wrestling match. He loved exaggeration and
dramatizing the obvious. "Guess who this is?" He placed two fingers
under his nose for a mustache, while extending his other arm in
a ramrod salute. Then he sang the Spike Jones spoof, "Right in Der
Fuhrer's Face." Dad hated dictators and never missed an opportunity to
mock Schiklgruber the Paperhanger.

Dad relished telling jokes from the pulpit, and in the privacy of
our little parsonage he laughed about the ludicrous aspects of his
profession. Ever hear about the preacher who lost his false teeth down
a well? Someone tied a drumstick to a string, lowered it into the well,
and up came the false teeth firmly attached. One time a backwoods
preacher spontaneously picked a verse to preach on, his finger landing
on the word "Nebuchadnezzar." "Well, I see here that old Nebo done
got hisself a razor," he extemporized. "Now I'm going to take that razor
and shave sin with it."

An elderly parishioner would sit in the back of the church and
grumble when Dad's sermons ran over the limit. She finally got so
vexed that she stood up and announced to everyone, "Drag, drag, drag!

17

I don't know about the rest of you, but I'm going home." Dad joked about it years afterward.

My parents gave me a sled for Christmas. I took it out for a trial run on the steep, snowy street in front of our parsonage. I pushed off, sliding faster and faster till my sled jerked to a stop on the gravelly pavement at the bottom, while I kept going face-first. Dad heard me yelping and ran out into the street, scooped me up, bloody mess that I was, and drove me to Mercy Hospital. In the room where they stitched my mouth, I noticed a crucifix on the wall, and in the vestibule something I had never seen before: a painting of the Virgin Mary. Though such images were alien to my Pentecostal upbringing, they did communicate to me something of the mysterious severity and gentleness of God.

Not long after, Mom gave birth to my sister Gay in the same hospital. I was so proud of my baby sister. How I loved to hold her in my arms. To this day she is a beloved confidante and friend.

The early 50s were a time of escalating terror. After we demonstrated our devastating power at Hiroshima and Nagasaki, the Soviets detonated their own atomic device in 1949. Now America and the Soviet Union were locked in a deadly race to produce an H-bomb.

Stalin died in 1953. Mom said, "They should drop a bomb on his grave." Half a year later as we sat by the tall, wooden radio in our living room, I listened to a firsthand description of the dropping of the first

American hydrogen bomb. "Ladies and gentlemen, look at all the colors! It's green. It's yellow. Now it's turning orange. Oh, this is spectacular!" The announcer went on and on about the test at Bikini Atoll, and we heard the whole thing on a Gothic-looking radio with wooden knobs.

ON THE SCENE

Three blocks from home on a summer night,
    shadows murmur under black trees,

"Mister Miller's had a heart attack."

Across the street, Miller Motors
    is going up in flames.

An orange cauldron boils
    into the sky;

a roof collapses, two firemen perish.

I'm seven years old, observing the world
    and its catastrophes.

Topeka

1954-55

WE MOVED to Topeka the year of Brown vs Board of Education. Dad thought he was called to be a healer. He believed he had supernatural power in his right hand, like Oral Roberts. He left Mom, my brother, sister and I with our grandparents and headed to California on a preaching tour. I remember a treasure he sent me from there—a papery, fine-nostriled seahorse, question-shaped, perfectly elegant. But something went wrong, nobody knows what. He finally gave up and came home.

Back in Topeka, Dad paced the floors. Loud noises infuriated him. He went into trances and talked to himself, wandered disoriented into traffic. No one could help him. One day, Grandpa Elvin caught him crawling out the attic window three stories up. That was the last straw. Grandpa said Dad must go to the hospital.

Dad was walking me to school one day in the rundown inner city. We stopped part-way, by a lilac hedge, bungalows in the background, common those days in old parts of Topeka. His crinkly black hair was combed straight back.

"Son, I'm having trouble with my nerves."

Dad had a ruddy complexion and aristocrat's nose. He wore creased slacks and a camel overcoat. "I can't handle my nerves. I have to go to a hospital."

I thought: No, Dad. Please don't be crazy.

He knelt down on the sidewalk, pulled me into the folds of his coat. I felt the fear in his chest. He held me close and said, "I love you, Stan." I stumbled in a blur the rest of the way to school as the green world disintegrated around me.

Mom went out to the state hospital to see what was left of her husband. She climbed the clanking steel stairs to the security ward. Dad was sitting in the corner. His right arm was wrapped in bandages, eyes glassed over, shirt soaking in drool. "Why did you come to see me?" he asked from far away. "I'm going to hell, anyway. Find another husband."

She sang to her husband, sang a song from the Spirit. Cradled him in her arms and sang, "God will take care of you."

Lincoln Elementary was a grim, three-story building in the inner city, surrounded by an asphalt playground and chain-link fence. Its first-floor windows glowered behind wire cages; an iron fire escape zagged down the outside. That's where I went to school while Dad was in the hospital.

After a month they moved me from second to third grade. It was a dazzling day for me because Mrs. Baca, my new teacher, had drawn a monarch butterfly on the blackboard with colored chalk, a majestic butterfly a hundred times bigger than life. I instantly loved Mrs. Baca with all my childish heart. What other glories awaited me in this third-grade classroom I couldn't imagine.

"Guess what," I told my neighborhood buddies. "I've been skipped to third grade." That meant little to them; they liked to shoot marbles and play war games. For some reason the conversation turned to wrestling. I said I could beat them both without using my arms. In a snap we were wallowing on the ground, and I soon had Billie, then Ronnie in gut-squashing scissor-holds with my legs. It surprised them as well as me.

Billie invited me to his house, a shanty wrapped in brick-patterned tarpaper, situated incongruously beside my grandfather's white house with its imperious eaves and columned porch; the two mismatched houses only a half-dozen steps apart. At Billie's the TV was going. Pinkie Lee had his hand stuck in a mailbox, a phony predicament. Silly clown. Billie's mom had a plaque in her kitchen: Everything I enjoy is either immoral, illegal, or fattening. She took her kids to the roller rink where they learned racy routines like the Bunny Hop, the sort of thing my family frowned on. Billie's dad was a railroad mechanic who loafed on the couch in his coveralls after work, his face wreathed in blissful fatigue. A dozen years after I knew him, Billie was killed in the jungles of Vietnam.

Grandpa's house had a spacious porch like a southern manse. Once I got my head stuck between the banisters and had to twist, oh, so carefully, to extricate myself. Someone had vandalized the porch's only furniture, a leather couch, by carving the word "fuck" into it, exposing the horsehair stuffing. Grandpa would sit out there with Mr. Griggs, an elderly boarder, the two talking politics and watching the sky for signs of a tornado. When low-hanging clouds curdled and turned yellow, that spelled trouble. A gigantic siren was situated just a few blocks away on a tall building in downtown Topeka. Its unearthly moan could signal one of two things: either an incoming tornado or a Soviet bomber and the end of the world.

◆

Mom worked hard as a clerk at the J. C. Penney store in downtown Topeka. We tried to have a good time as best we could without Dad. I remember sitting on the back steps at Grandpa's house with my brother Brent, staring at the long strip of dirt and weeds that served as our playground—the same back yard where Mom had played as a girl. At the end sat a dilapidated garage, beyond that an alley, and a block or so further down a wooded hill, the Acheson, Topeka & Santa Fe railroad tracks. A block the other direction was the Negro neighborhood. "When will we see Dad again?" Brent asked me. That was an unanswerable question, but I assured my little brother we'd see him soon. Brent had been damaged at birth—nearly strangled on his own umbilical cord—and was developing slower than other children.

Two big deals at Grandpa Elvin's house: the Saturday Night Fights and Texas Wrestling; one deadly earnest, the other farcical. When the wrestlers came on, Grandpa fastened his gleaming eyes on their carnivalesque antics, and none of us dared move. How he could be duped by the choreographed wrestling matches escaped me, but I had no doubts about the authenticity of the weekly prize fights, which sought with asperity week by week to resolve the question: who's the toughest guy in the jungle?

Grandpa Elvin, a big-boned Swede, had been raised on a farm in northern Kansas, the youngest of eleven children, hence his name, meaning "number eleven." He got pampered by doting sisters, but his older brothers liked to knock him around, so he was perpetually looking for ways to even the score. I suppose he was looking for some kind of vicarious fulfillment when he put me up to a fist fight with my neighbor buddies, Billie and Ronnie. The scene: the asphalted, sagging alleyway behind Grandpa's house, lined by fences, smelly trashcans, garages, and upspringing sumacs. Grandpa had the three of us corralled there. I didn't know what to expect. Then his booming voice commanded me to attack. Without thinking I charged at my friend Ronnie and slammed him in the nose. To my amazement, blood splurted out as he fell to the pavement. In disbelief I ran to a corner of the alley, curled into a ball, and cried.

Yes, and it was in this selfsame alley I saw the strange, horrible photographs of the Hungarian Revolution (why didn't we help them?), read comic-book versions of *A Tale of Two Cities* and the life of President Lincoln (Sarah Todd threw his proffered rose to the dirt; he sunk into melancholia. A new thought—melancholia, strange sickness—), and met Rhea, dear redheaded Rhea, who fell headfirst down the stairwell at Lincoln Elementary and died.

◆

We're in the packed Municipal Auditorium listening to a wraithlike lady with bright, sunken eyes tell about her sojourn in hell. To skeptics she's no doubt describing a schizophrenic episode, but we, the committed and faithful, hang onto every word as evidence of a reality just beyond our grasp. She describes the torment in such vivid detail that we can hardly bear it. At one point in her nightmarish experience she had thrust a straight pin through her hand to see if she was still alive, but felt no pain. Her thin voice crackles with conviction. She's been there. She knows. "I implore you, turn to Jesus now while you have the opportunity."

Another speaker raked us over the coals, thundering on about There's somebody in this auditorium tonight. You know who you are.

If you walk out of here without making a decision for Christ, you will never have another chance. God has revealed to me that someone is going to step out these doors and pass into eternity this very night. It may have been true for all I know, but to me it felt like manipulation. What made it worse was the way he scalded us with the fear of committing the unpardonable sin.

Return to Paradise

1957

THREE YEARS LATER, Dad was out of the hospital. He spent several months in occupational rehabilitation learning the upholstery trade and managed to run a hog ring through his finger. He thought he could do better as a house painter. The call of Durango was strong, and we soon had packed up the Studebaker for a return to southwestern Colorado, where life had been reasonably good before his nervous breakdown. At first it would be just Dad and me. Later the rest of the family would join us.

As we pulled out of the backyard, Grandpa told my father, "You'll never make it." Grandpa didn't have a lot of faith in Dad, and he didn't have much use for Colorado, either. He once said, "What good are mountains? You can't raise wheat on them."

Dad and I rolled out of Topeka and headed west. By the end of the day we had most of the wheat behind us. The next morning I rolled down the window and let out a yip as we sailed into Colorado. When we stopped for gas in Alamosa, Dad bought me a jumbo postcard featuring a rectangular Colorado five times bigger than all the other miniscule states huddled around it. A cheeky cowgirl on the card yodeled, "Why-oh-why did I ever leave 'Yoming?" To come to Colorful Colorado, that's why! A cow grinned with crazy teeth, and a trout leaped out of the water. Splash. I ran my finger along the postcard's ripply edge. A knob-kneed goat balanced atop an ice cream cone mountain, and the cowgirl kept on yodeling.

We pulled into Durango that evening. Perrins Peak gazed down on the dusty town like a sphinx. Pinyon forests spilled over peach-colored cliffs above the town. Little frame houses smothered by cottonwoods squatted in the valley bottom. Brick store fronts lined Main Street, dominated by a grand hotel laced with silver-painted corbels and cornices. This was not Topeka. There were no massive public edifices of granite, no capitol dome, no tornado sirens. We had returned to the American West.

Dad found work right away painting tract houses for a contractor named Barton. I was free to do what I pleased. Sometimes I hung around the subdivision on the west side of town. Other times I'd go exploring in the arroyos at the foot of Perrins Peak.

I bought a first aid kit at the army surplus store. Its oily-smelling canvas pockets were tucked full of gauze bandages, burn ointment and safety pins. It also had glass vials of merthiolate sewn into cloth tubes. If you got cut you snapped the vial in two, and the stinging red tincture oozed out.

"Dad, I'm going up into the hills. I've got my first aid kit and canteen."

"Okay. Be back before quitting time."

Up the pinyon-dotted hills I clambered, following loose shale ridges and ravines. The air was pungent with sagebrush. My shoes filled with dirt; my socks bagged up. Exotic junipers sprang into the air, cinnamon bark hanging in shreds from their twisted trunks. I sat and emptied my shoes and socks, then rose to clamber on. A short while later I stopped again. At my feet lay a large round clump of dry mud. It was inexplicably symmetrical, gray, and shaped like a lovely tortoise shell. I stared in amazement at this strange artifact for which I had no name. When I picked it up, it crumbled to pieces.

I caught Dad in time for supper. We sauntered into a café on Main Street, bellied up to the counter and ordered hamburgers and Cokes. It was an up-and-coming cafe with shiny Formica countertop and padded swivel stools. Along the counter were chrome-trimmed plastic boxes with hit songs typed on index cards. I flipped through the choices: "Tumbling Tumbleweeds" by the Sons of the Pioneers, "Blueberry Hill," "Mule Train." Romantic stuff by dames with big lipsticky mouths.

I put my nickel in the slot and punched the ruby-red buttons for G-2, "All Shook Up." A little stage hung above the dining area. The curtain jerked open, then flannel-clothed marionettes began to play.

Elvis moaned and cajoled and appealed to something primal in me which, like the tortoise shell, I had no name for.

The drummer flailed stiffly with his sticks, bobbing up and down at the waist. The singer turned his head from side to side with a perpetual smile. Presley was in a tizzy—shuddering from the belly, in the throes of love. The pianist flagellated the little fake piano. The bassist rocked back and forth. I dug Elvis. He grabbed me. I couldn't help it.

After supper, Dad and I strolled the dark streets of Durango and paused at a lighted store window, where an oil painting was on display. Ghostly faces stared out the back of a cargo truck. A title card tacked to the easel said, We Are Going. Where were they going, to a labor camp? For years after that, whenever our family headed out the door on some grand excursion, Dad would arch his eyebrows and announce quixotically, "We are going."

Dad made a hundred dollars a week working for Barton. He wore baggy white overalls hanging from white straps on his shoulders. He'd push the roller on a long "pogo stick" into the tray of paint, then lift it over his head, rolling out the ceiling, his curly black hair and Roman nose immersed in clouds of damp fumes.

Once I decided to play a trick on him by dropping a wad of lint into his roller pan and waiting for him to roll it onto the ceiling. Mid-track he noticed the lint, plucked it off the ceiling and flicked it away.

I sidled to the corner where it landed, retrieved it and dropped it back into the pan when Dad wasn't looking, then suppressed a ripple of glee as he hoisted it overhead again. I could barely contain myself. Dad reached up and picked it out of the wet paint a second time, more than a little aggravated, not realizing I was the culprit.

Then came the evening we left Durango to pick up Mom and my brother and sister at the bus depot in Albuquerque. Dad and I got lost, going a hundred miles out of our way in the black of night somewhere in New Mexico. By the time we got to them, they'd sat up most of the night waiting for us. They looked like an immigrant family all huddled together wrapped in blankets.

Coming back from Albuquerque as the Studebaker rounded the last curve, we encountered a roadblock. People were gathered under a banner reading, "KIUP Radio Welcomes You to Durango." The next thing we knew a guy with a broad grin flagged us off the road. He sported a fancy western shirt and bolo tie and had a microphone in his hand. Dad rolled down the window. The radio announcer poked his head into our car and asked, "What brings you to the scenic San Juans?"

"We'd rather not comment," Dad answered, memories of the hospital fresh in his mind. Then we crested the hill and rolled down into paradise.

We moved into a Barton show home on the west edge of town. Our job was to model the suburban life for prospective buyers. But Topeka haunted us. Sometimes Dad joked about the nuthouse with cyanide humor. His brain had been cauterized forty-eight times—blank continents for memory. His right arm crawled with angry red worms. There was no hair anywhere on that arm from forearm to fingertips, scalded. Seventeen long years would elapse before a clue to his mysterious burnt arm would emerge in the form of a devastating memory recall. For now, it lurked like a monster in the unknowable depths.

Dad was a regular clown. He played guitar, dashed bright oil paints on the canvas. But, off-moments, he fixed an eye on that arm. And when he did, it shook and trembled with a mind of its own. He stared, fascinated. So did I.

I brought home a puppy. Dad bought me a pellet gun. Sometimes I took the gun out to a field and shot at prairie dogs. Navajos herded sheep through the sagebrush behind our house. In Topeka I had become fascinated with Indians while frequenting the State Historical Museum; we lived only four blocks away. The parfleches and quivers, the perfect beadwork moccasins, taut buffalo-hide shields, bone breastplates and tomahawks, lances and arrows, a scalp with thick black hair and a clot of dried skin—these clung to me like a green bur.

Now that I had landed in Indian country, that bur sprouted into an obsession. I made bonnets and bustles of bright plumage ordered from the *Grey Owl Catalogue.* Tufts of down drifted into the corners of our model suburban home. My workbench might be a kitchen chair or the coffee table as I sliced and sewed. Ben Hunt's *Book of Indian Crafts and Lore* was always opened to some new project.

I learned the tribal names and ordered authentic recordings of war chants and love songs. Ben Hunt's book contained diagrams of red and black moccasin tracks showing the various dance steps. I learned to trace arcs with my toes. ONE two three four. Pivoting, stalking, only touching down with the ball of my foot. There was a spring-loaded dance step, ONE-two ONE-two, which launched me into exultation. I bobbed and pranced with elastic legs faster and faster and faster. "You never put your foot down when you walk," Dad observed. "You go everywhere on the balls of your feet." I was proud he noticed.

The first time we'd lived in Durango, I had a little girlfriend named Vicki. She was Navajo, but had been adopted by white parents. We had passed pleasant hours together listening to children's stories on her record player. I wrote to Vicki from Topeka to tell her we were coming back, but she didn't answer my letter. I looked her up when we got to Durango. "You can't expect girls her age to write back," her mother said. Our friendship resumed seamlessly. We made acorn cakes under the gambel oaks. This time when she played a record for me, it was Jim Dandy to the Rescue. She liked the beat and wanted to know if I liked it, too.

Vicki had shiny black hair and dimples and a full, soft smile. I asked her if she would march with me in the Fiesta Days parade. Yes, she would. She wore a brown squaw dress, a beaded headband, and a white feather plaited into her lustrous pigtail. I wore orange plumed arm bustles with mirrors in the center and ankle bells and a black felt loin cloth. Vicki walked along beside me in her dignified way. I leaped and pranced, playing to the crowd on Main Street. Spring-step. Staying on the balls of my feet.

Now that our family had been repatriated to paradise, we went exploring. Dad chauffeured us around the Four Corners, intent on capturing as much of the countryside as possible with his camera. We traveled north over Molas Divide to the austere, half-abandoned mining town of Silverton, then south through rugged scrublands to the Navajo reservation, where squaws wore velveteen skirts and bright blouses festooned with turquoise jewelry. Dad photographed the narrow-gage train winding through the gorges of the Animas River, aspen shadows on the snow, facades of abandoned buildings, the pageantry and hoopla of the rodeo parade, sky-searing sunsets, mud hogans, and reticent, weather-beaten squaws.

He staged family events, slide shows, featuring platters of yummies: crackers, blue cheese, olives, and smoked oysters ("urs durvs") served with a feast for the eyes—luminous scenes on the magic screen. Dad had a cardboard box of slides bundled with rubber bands. Each bundle bristled with subjects for lively chatter: Wolf Creek Pass, Aztec Ruins, Million Dollar Highway, Rodeo Days.

A bright green meadow appeared on the screen, shimmering in front of jet black hills. Dad declared, "If you painted a scene like that, people would say you made it up." Then the room filled with the glow of naked sandstone cliffs and stone-hewn ruins. Ah, Mesa Verde. The Anasazi built their homes here, grew corn, beans and squash on the mesas, took shelter under gigantic arches of sandstone. I wanted to know all about them.

Our family had visited various ruins around the Four Corners. Mother especially shared my enthusiasm for the ancient people. We marveled at the black and white designs on their pottery, their cubist architecture. We mused about their mysterious exodus from the clifflands in 1300 A.D. Dad enjoyed these things too, but he was there mainly for the open spaces and raw color.

I wrote a letter to park headquarters.

> Dear Sir:
> I have heard that they are going to excavate some more ruins. Would you be interested in taking a ten year old boy (me) along with you? I am a good climber, and fairly good at archeology. I could carry packs or something for you, just so I could go along. I hope to be an archeologist when I grow up.

The superintendent declined my offer. He suggested that I could be of assistance after acquiring a college degree. I thought his response was unimaginative and condescending.

That fall I began fifth grade at Needham Elementary. I asked a girl who was sitting on the merry-go-round, "Are there any kids at this school who are interested in Indians?" She rolled her eyes and answered, "They sure act like a bunch of wild Indians." And she was right. Crazed-eyed boys chased girls around the playground, trapping them in corners so they could kiss them. Mother taught me at an early age to save my kisses for my wife. Promiscuous kissing, as practiced by the scalawags at Needham Elementary, was just plain nasty.

There was a girl in our class named Mary Clark, who was no scalawag. Mary was a dusky-skinned beauty with hair as dark as charred butternut. She wore it short. Mary had proportion, social and intellectual, to the same degree the rest of us lacked it. She was of decidedly superior upbringing. I didn't have a crush on her or anything like that, but I was in awe of her.

At Halloween I was invited to my first Needham Elementary social affair, a party at the home of Charlene Miller, the springy-haired blonde who had rolled her eyes on the merry-go-round. I went dressed as Elvis Presley. It didn't take long before we were playing the guessing game. All the boys jammed into a large closet and took turns guessing whose voice was on the other side of the door. "Stan, it's your turn," they told me. "What happens if he guesses right?" they asked the girls. "We'll tell after he guesses," the girls answered.

The mystery person spoke, and it was no mystery to me. That was Mary Clark's voice. "It's Mary's." Female titterings on the other side of the door. One of the girls squealed, "He has to kiss her."

As the door opened, I threw myself in panic against the back wall of the closet. "You have to do it." Six boys grabbed me and shoved me toward the open door. I just about climbed right out of their hands and straight up to the ceiling. "I can't. Kissing is nasty." They might just as well have tried to pull my pants down in the middle of a baseball stadium. I wasn't going to kiss Mary Clark, and that was all there was to it.

There was a vacant lot full of weeds behind the school which served as a battleground for the fifth and sixth grade boys. I don't remember any boys not participating. Half stood at one end of the field—it really didn't matter which side you were on—and half at the other. We pulled up heavy clumps of dirt by their long weed-handles, swung them over our heads and heaved them at the other side. Such hooting and howling, such exultation when a clod collided with the enemy. Such taunting when someone missed. We were having the time of our lives. Let the girls play hopscotch. We were mud-daubed savages engaged in a primeval occupation. The whole thing came to a halt when a kid got hit in the eye and went crying to the principal.

But there were other splendid battles fought after school and on weekends, in thickets away from the eyes of teachers, where we could throw ourselves against one another in wild abandon, wooden swords crashing against garbage can lids for shields, pummeling each other lustily to the ground. And there was the fight I had with Kenny on his front lawn when I pounded his face and knocked a tooth loose.

There was a near-fight the following year, in sixth grade. Convinced that some students enjoyed privileged treatment at our school, I organized a counter movement called the Plebeians. We shunned popular kids at recess. A Plebeian girl brought home-baked goodies to share with Plebeian boys. This led to a showdown between Danny Grumman, champion of the Patricians, and me, champion of the downtrodden. Danny was handsome, popular, tanned, athletic. When the time came for a fight, he made a show of putting on leather dress gloves so he wouldn't damage his hands while pounding me to a pulp. Then he leaped into the air, spun around, ran up to the school wall, pushed off it, and finally attacked me. At that moment the recess bell rang and cut the whole thing short.

Soon afterward, the principal marched into our classroom and delivered a scalding lecture on the evils of social stratification. We would have to lay prejudice aside and adopt a tolerant attitude—this was how society worked. We had better learn it now. Furthermore, announced the principal, she had no respect for rabble-rousers. I rode my bike home that afternoon in a sour mood, talking to myself.

Back in fifth grade, things had gone along well enough. We learned our states and capitals, long division and all. The wonderful thing about that year was that Mom and Dad, poor as they were, provided me with private art lessons. I had the good fortune to receive art instruction from Chickie Heuser, wife of a professor at Fort Lewis College. She had a pure, lovely face, black hair braided in pigtails, and dark friendly eyes. A handful of grade school students attended her classes on Saturday mornings.

Chickie taught us that every composition must have a center of interest, a compelling focus. That there must be contrast: for example, a dab of orange somewhere in a field of green. That a certain amount of repetition is pleasing to the soul.

We learned the value scale: black (the absence of color), white (all colors of the rainbow), and shades of gray. We learned the color wheel, hues melting together in a mouthwatering blur as you circumnavigated the mystical chart. On its outer edge loomed dark hues like forest green and midnight blue. Then, dominating the chart, a jeweled band of bright color: amethyst, vermilion, citron yellow, glowing orange, pure blue. Moving inward, these dissolved into a whirlpool of pastels, which in turn gave way to omnivorous white. We experimented with brushes and paints on paper. Sometimes we made mud, other times we mixed the most wonderful, exotic shades. Dusty rose, peach, avocado, magenta. We exulted as the colors flowed from our paintbrushes.

Chickie taught us complements, full of surprise and delight. Mint green with dark maroon. Deep violet with banana cream yellow. Opposites like these showed each other off to advantage.

Chickie took us to a ballet class to draw the human figure in motion. We visited art exhibits, attended a play, learned perspective, and copied old masterpieces. She taught us so many things. And she accepted me. I loved her dearly.

◆

On my eleventh birthday I became a Boy Scout. I got to hang out with older, rougher boys who shoved each other around and brayed like donkeys. This was intoxicating stuff for me. Our troop leader was Mr. Turner, a hard-nosed drill sergeant who punished infractions by sending us through the swat line.

Everything was dead serious. You'd better know how to resuscitate somebody you've just dragged out of the water. You'd better know what to do for sprained ankles, puncture wounds, poison ivy, and compound fractures; how to carry someone out of a burning building; how to signal an airplane if you're lost in the woods; how to lash poles together with good, sturdy lashing. And be ready with a "Yes, sir!" and a snappy salute for Mr. Turner. Did I love this? I thrived on it.

Dad wasn't much of a disciplinarian. A comrade, yes, but something in me hungered for the stirring exactitude of Mr. Turner's commands. Line up! Atten–SHUN. About FACE. You spun on the balls of your feet just so. Forward, MARCH. HEP two-three-four. If you did it right, you had his respect. If you were a slouch—well, that wasn't tolerated.

We played this crazy game called Ditch 'em, which to my mind is one of the greatest games ever invented, right up there with broomball and chess. After Turner drilled and marched us around awhile, we'd divide into teams, hunters and hunted. The hunted scattered like rabbits into bushes, hillocks and crannies as dusk settled over the large schoolyard that served as our playing field. The hunters, after counting a hundred, came loping into the gloom, on the alert, panting hard. They had to spot you, chase you down, tag you—then you went to jail until someone busted you out. The hunted crouched low, barely breathing.

Once I climbed up into a juniper tree and stood on a branch maybe half an hour, listening to the sounds of the chase. At one point a hunter paused at the base of my tree but never looked up. I stayed there until the game was over.

Animas Valley

1958

FOUR CORNERS country overflowed with relics. I used to swoop my bike up and down an ancient kiva a few blocks from our house. Every time we went to Mesa Verde I studied the splendorous array of artifacts at the visitor center: yucca sandals, arrowheads, blankets of juniper bark, spears, shapely pots. Always I gravitated to a glass case enclosing a stunningly preserved mummy named Esther. I was fascinated by her taut parchment-like skin, her leathery breasts, her exposed gums and teeth, her coarse black hair, knees drawn tightly to her chest.

Once, Dad drove us to a beanfield north of Cortez, where pottery lay everywhere on the ground. I lost myself immediately in the nearest arroyo, got down on my hands and knees and sifted through the debris. Picking up this piece and that, I noticed that some shards were corrugated, while others were smooth and decorated with black lines painted onto a white background. I could see fingerprints on the corrugated pieces. An ancient woman had formed this pot between her hands. Pat-a-pat. How old were the concentric ridges made by her fingertips? They couldn't be dated like tree rings.

I kept my potsherds and arrowheads in a compact box of hammered brass. I had found them all in that rock-rimmed arroyo strewn with rabbit brush. Not least among my treasures was a Folsom point, or it would have been a point if the point hadn't been broken off. It was oval-shaped, with shallow grooves on both faces, smooth between my thumb and forefinger, fashioned of translucent white quartz with a transverse black stripe. A lovely heirloom, even if broken.

I kept that box for many years until it finally disappeared.

♦

Chickie, my art teacher, started a day camp called the Galloping Goose. She and her professor-husband and children lived at the mouth of a side canyon halfway up the Animas Valley in a ramshackle cabin— not exactly the ivy-covered brick cottage one might expect. Here, at Galloping Goose "headquarters," she provided archery lessons, horseback riding, arts and crafts, hands-on science projects (Indian headdresses? clinker gardens?) and—so magnanimous of her—hired me to guide her campers up the canyon path behind her house. I reveled in my role as a professional "guide."

Chickie took me to a chamber of commerce meeting. "What Durango needs," I told them, "is a way to promote itself as an authentic western town." I had in mind old-style store fronts on Main Street, maybe boardwalks and horse-drawn carriages, definitely gunfights with stuntmen stumbling into the gutters, barbecues, Indian dances.

"We're so pleased you came," said the old heads around the table in the dark-paneled room. "It's not every day a 10-year-old contributes an item to our agenda." In another 10 years I would receive a bemused letter from Peter Dominick, senior Senator from Colorado, musing, "It's not every day I hear from one of my zapped constituents."

Chickie was pleased with herself for bringing me to the chamber meeting. She was always up to something. Out on the street she showed me a mural she had painted in a department store window (she was the official window dresser) and dared me to find the word "potrzebie" hidden in it. A Navajo man came out a tavern door clutching a pair of shattered eyeglasses to his chest and weeping like a child. We might not have been a "western town" in the Disneyesque sense, but Durango did have its peculiar charms.

After a year of living in town, my family moved to a cobblestone house way up the Animas Valley. A creek ran by; ponderosas blanketed the valley in piney perfume. I built a sweat lodge by the creek. A half-mile away, the Animas River boiled under Baker's Bridge, site of a dramatic shootout scene in The Naked Spur. That winter I ran through the snowy ponderosa forest stripped to the waist, convinced I was an Indian. This was Eden.

Christmas in the cobblestone house was the best ever. Dad dressed up like Santa Claus and came jingling up to the door, yo-ho-hoed, pulled his beard off and announced, "Do you know who Santa is? He's your own sweet Daddy." Mom had fudge cooling in the snow. The pungency of fresh-cut spruce filled the house. The tree was festooned with bubbling, incandescent "candles" and plumed birds of fine-blown glass. We played Rocket Ship, our favorite game, in which Dad leaned a mattress against the wall, lay on his back with legs cocked, and catapulted us through the air. The sheer mad joy.

◆

"Hop in the car," says Dad, "we're going to the dump." Toodle-oo. We're off on a gentlemen's errand – to throw away rags and paint cans and dried-up roller skins, and so much more importantly, to scrounge in the lowdown dump. What would a fine-looking man like my father be doing in a place like that, with an odor to make you gag? He'd be up to his elbows in glee, sifting through the flotsam, looking for that special something. Perhaps this goes back to his fruit-picking days when discards were treasure, when he and Grandma lived in a tent, counting every blessing. Dad and I make a pair as we tromp through the trash. Such ecstasy!—to salvage what's on the verge of perishing.

We rumble merrily home along a dirt road, Dad energetically expounding on 1930s culture and teaching me to sing "Ragtime Cowboy Joe."

Wet Behind the Ears

1964

OUTWARD BOUND – what an experience. I'd read about it in *Reader's Digest*, applied, gotten a scholarship from Gates Rubber. I was barely shaving, didn't know how to drive a car, and had never been on a date, but at the end of this twenty-seven-day course they would give me a "man badge." I arrived with a busload of teenage boys in July, 1964, at the dilapidated quarry town of Marble, Colorado. We hiked up a steep gravel road to the school, situated in an aspen forest three miles above the town.

The school, like me, was wet behind the ears, having been established just two years before. It was directed by Joe Nold, who had taught at the prestigious Gordonstoun School, Prince Charles's alma mater. Five patrols of boys, sixty lads in all, gathered in a grassy amphitheater around a blazing campfire that first evening as Nold welcomed us to the course in his clipped, aristocratic diction. He was imposing, though short, with the visage of an eagle. He contrasted our sheltered suburban lives with Thoreau's rustic experiment at Walden Pond, challenging us with these words:

Wet Behind the Ears

I went to the woods because I wished to live deliberately,

to front only the essential facts of life, and see if I could

not learn what it had to teach, and not, when I came to

die, discover that I had not lived.

So this was our task at Outward Bound: to reduce life to the basics: food, warmth and survival. To get "mud on our shoes and feel the wind on our faces," as Nold put it. We would be tested mentally and physically, and endure. I was ready for it. Though immature in many ways, I was on friendly terms with the mountains, having already bagged some peaks. I had taught mountaineering classes for the Colorado Mountain Club that spring and had climbed an easy route up the east face of Long's Peak two weeks before the course began.

I slept in a canvas shepherd's tent that night. These were set on wooden platforms and furnished with cots. At six our patrol instructor roused us out of the sack for a half-mile run and frigid dip in Lost Trail Creek. Chilled to the bone, I ran back to camp in sloshing wet tennis shoes and crawled into the sleeping bag to catch some more sleep. Herb Kincey, my instructor, came into the tent and informed me there would be no slacking. Welcome to Outward Bound.

After the clanking of a cowbell and a moment of silence, breakfast was served in the dining hall. We polished off generous helpings of scrambled eggs, bacon and toast, washing it down with hot cocoa. All of this tasted fine after the morning run and dip. Then our patrol, the Nez Perces, assembled at the ropes course – a wonderful complex of swings, bridges, cargo nets and ladders strung fancifully among the aspens. In this open-air arena we swooped like Tarzan through the trees, hooted like chimpanzees, embarked on desperate commando missions. We negotiated a high-swung Burma bridge, feeling the buoyancy of rope beneath our feet, the delicious pull of gravity. Sunlight dappled our faces; shouts reverberated through the aspen grove. Elegant white trunks, blotched with black, shot into the alpine sky as jade-and-silver leaves fluttered and shimmered overhead.

A twenty-foot log leaned diagonally against a tree, with notches cut into it for steps. I ascended the notches, confidently at first, then more precariously, arms waving and hips swaying for balance, pushing through a threshold of fear before reaching the top.

We attacked the wall, a twelve-foot-high obstacle fashioned of smooth planks. The object was to get everyone over the top as quickly as possible. Two stout patrol members grabbed a third one and pushed him up the blank wall till he could grasp the top. He clambered up, then reached down to help the next. It became a mad scramble as we raced against the clock. Patrol mates were hauled up by their britches and armpits, thumping and bumping against the wide planks as they struggled to the top. The next to last fellow lowered himself back over the wall like a human ladder, with several mates holding onto his arms and shoulders for dear life. The last man ran for it, leaped up, grabbed a pant leg, then clambered for the fellow's waist, nearly pulling his trousers off, then latched onto his shirt, toes scuffing at the boards while hands reached down to grab him. Everybody heaved, and both fellows came over the top at the same time. Did we trounce the other patrols? We looked eagerly to Herb, who just shook his head and said we could do better next time.

In the afternoon they issued us equipment from the commissary, laughably primitive by today's standards: combat boots which were to be kept limber and waterproof with a smelly substance called Neatsfoot Oil; wool socks, wool pants, and a scratchy, olive drab wool shirt; a long, wooden-handled Austrian ice axe which doubled as a walking stick; an army surplus wooden pack frame guaranteed to rub your shoulders raw; and a 12x12 sheet of plastic which would serve as a tent for a cook group of three students. I can't remember all the gear, but that was some of it.

There was spaghetti and a big salad for supper, after the cowbell and moment of silence. The fellow who jangled the bell also played a banjo. He was a couple of years older than us, and wore striped suspenders. As we were finishing supper, he led us in singing "Where Have All the Flowers Gone," a protest song made popular by the Kingston Trio. Every month, more troops were being deployed to Vietnam.

Then a burly bear of a man with gigantic bushy eyebrows stood up to speak. He wore a plaid lumberjack shirt and wool army pants. This was Paul Petzoldt, the climbing legend. He began his career in 1924 by ascending the Grand Teton in cowboy boots. This adolescent stunt nearly cost him his life. Sobered by this first experience, he became a student of the mountains and learned to ply his craft skillfully and safely. He became the first guide in the Tetons, then distinguished himself on the American expedition to K-2 in 1938 by climbing to an altitude of 26,000 feet without oxygen. In World War II he trained 10th Mountain Division ski troops at Camp Hale. Now he stood before us as Outward Bound's chief climbing instructor.

I already had my pantheon of climbing heroes, Hermann Buhl and Layton Kor among others, but here was a live one standing right in front of me. Mirth rippled under the boulder field of his gruff voice as he expounded on his love affair with the high, wild places of the earth. Why did he spend so much time way up there, on the rocky heights? "So I can appreciate my valley friends better." He spoke to us from his deep store of experience, emphasizing sound judgment as the key to enjoying the out-of-doors. Don't take foolish chances. "There are old mountaineers and there are bold mountaineers," he intoned, "but there are no old, bold mountaineers." Then he confided, "I want to be known as the OLD man of the mountains." He was in fine form that night. An ancient oak among saplings, Petzoldt communicated to us his grand enthusiasm for life. Yeah, I wanted that, too. To be a mountain man, to spend my life in the wild places.

The next morning I got to wrestle with that wooly bear. He sat us on the ground in front of the commissary and drilled us on belaying technique. I'd already had that drummed into me at climbing school. I knew the right way and wrong way to belay. I had even caught some long falls on the Mountain Club towers, and was proud of my technique. But Petzoldt took exception to it. He came bustling up behind me while I maneuvered the rope, wrapped his big arms around my waist and started jostling the rope in a helter-skelter fashion. "That's the way we do it," he growled. I thought, there's no sense arguing with him; this must be the way they did it in the thirties.

The next few days passed rapidly, with lessons in axemanship and firefighting, an airy free-hanging rappel off a cliff overlooking Lizard Lake, and snow-climbing practice in Grizzly Basin. We learned the mountain pace and acquired a sense of ease in navigating the forests and ridges surrounding the school. We hiked everywhere, trails or not. Our instructor, Herb Kincey, read inspirational passages to us each morning. "Now, fellas," he said, "here is something to think about." Then he crooned the words to us in his velvet North Carolina drawl:

If you think you are beaten, you are:

If you think you dare not you won't.

If you like to win but don't think you can

It's almost certain you won't

If you think you'll lose, you're lost;

For out in the world you'll find

Success begins with a fellow's will;

It's all in a state of mind.

I listened, mesmerized as the message crept into my soul. Herb was imparting a vital lesson, the essential Outward Bound philosophy. I admired Herb for sharing these morning readings with us, and began to esteem him like my own father.

Life's battles don't always go

To the stronger or faster man,

But sooner or later, the man who wins

Is the fellow who thinks he can.

After several days of camp-based training, we launched into the wilds. Herb guided us up Whitehouse Mountain, our patrol locking into gear and chugging up the steep, untracked east flank. We picked our steps, moving as a unit, threading our way up cliff bands and talus, through grassy ledges and meadows. It was exhilarating to travel this way, savoring the freedom of the hills. We trod on brittle stones. Several times I found myself on the threshold of some primeval sanctuary, an archway of chokecherries, say, opening into a verdant chamber of feathery bracken ferns and soft moss and tall green grass. So surprising a welcome.

We topped out on a narrow saddle and picked our way down the sprawling west flank, passing by a broad stripe of snow-white marble and the deserted Strauss Quarry. At the bottom lay Yule Quarry, source of marble for the Lincoln Memorial and Tomb of the Unknown Soldier. Before us loomed a gray-white escarpment into which three square caverns had been gouged—ancient it seemed, as the Valley of the Kings. We scrambled up a jumble of giant stone blocks to one of the caverns and stood at the edge and peered in. Remnants of wooden stairs clung to overhanging walls, promising destruction to any fool who tried to climb them. Beneath: cold, black water and hard ice.

Our patrol wound its way up the narrow Yule valley: a wet, primitive Eden. Thimbleberries hung over the trail. We tramped in black mud, picking our way from stone to stone where the trail pooled with water. We brushed past tall bushes from which I plucked a handful of sweet succulent berries. Here and there a root wriggled across the path. Pine scent saturated the air. Then the narrow valley opened unexpectedly into a wide meadow, and we were accosted by butterflies. We had arrived at Thompson Flat. Herb set some students out, one at a time, in isolated dells along the edge of the spacious meadow, then moved past it into dark, steep timber, continuing to drop us off. This part of the course was known as the solo.

My turn came. The place was unattractive, hemmed in by tall trees. I would spend the next three days here alone with nothing to eat. I unrolled my bag and sat until evening, then crawled in and watched the stars pass over the tops of the trees. Next morning I was hungry and looked around for something to eat. I rolled over a rock and found ants underneath, so I started eating the eggs. That's all I could find. The white doughy lozenges tasted like pastry. I got pretty weak, since I weighed only a hundred and twenty pounds. I wandered halfheartedly within the area Herb had marked out. No berries anywhere. Just imperious Doug firs with rough brown trunks looming up, their low dead branches useless to me without a match to start a fire. I filled a billycan with water from a slow-flowing brooklet, then lay in my sack for the next couple of days. The forest around me looked flat, impassive. Horseflies landed in the can of water and turned it bitter, but I drank it anyway, unwilling to venture out of the bag for more.

Herb came and picked me up the morning after my third night out. It had been a dreary experience. He asked me what I had gained from my time alone, and I told him there was nothing significant. I rolled up my bag and followed him down Yule Creek to his camp where my patrol mates had already gathered around a leaping fire. A large cast-iron griddle sizzled on the coals, and the savory smell of crackling bacon tweaked our noses. There were piles of pancakes waiting, and we saturated them with syrup and stuffed our faces full of them and drank soothing draughts of hot cocoa and staggered around like drunks and collapsed in the grass with bulging bellies.

Herb put up with that for a short while, then rousted us to our feet. We put out the fire and slung on our packs. No time for loafing. We were marching back to school on the double. I did all right the first few miles, but when we hit the long uphill I started to flag. The guys kicked it in gear and pushed along, but I had no reserve. The steep, hot dusty road crawled under my feet. Scrub oaks swam around me. My body seized up and refused to function. "This is hell," I thought, then fainted in my tracks. Herb had me stay put. A half-hour later a Jeep came down to fetch me, and I suffered the ignominy of being transported to camp.

We rested for a day, then headed out on the Grand Alpine Expedition as a rugged mountain-ready group. We saw many eye-dazzling sights the first day: a lacy waterfall on Lost Trail Creek, fields of avalanche lilies below Mount Daly, and a grassy unnamed ridge sweeping from Mount Richey to the upper Avalanche Basin. We camped somewhere along that luxuriant green ridge and feasted on whistle pig and wild mushrooms for supper—Herb carried a collapsible rifle in his pack.

We traversed the majestic ridge next day and dropped down to Avalanche Lake, which served as rendezvous for several patrols. A steep cliff beside the lake provided a venue for friendly climbing competition, a challenge my fingers itched for. I slithered up the stone like a lizard, hot and eager. Oh, that delicious feeling—try and slow me down. An English climbing instructor, Tony Greenbank, was there. He had a long reach, but the route foiled him. He was displeased that a mere student had out-climbed him. Of course that went straight to my head, but it turned out that Tony was coming down with tick fever.

The next day took us up a zigzag trail to a high pass. Herb had a standing rule that we would do pushups in a cold mountain stream if we were late getting started on the trail in the morning. On this day we had been late, but smugly assumed there was no way he could enforce his rule so far above timberline with nothing but tundra in sight. Then we came over that austere pass and looked down into a rocky bowl where icebergs floated in the indigo water of Capitol Lake. At an altitude of 12,000 feet, with the wind whistling, we stripped to bare skin and leaped into the arctic water. I shot out of that water like a rocket and thrashed wildly to shore, roaring with sheer delight as waves of golden warmth came pouring over me. Nobody stayed in long enough for pushups. Our whooping and bellowing bounced off the north face of Capitol Peak towering overhead.

By late afternoon we had ascended to 13,000 feet on the east side of the peak, where we removed our heavy packs in a sea of saucer-shaped rocks, a place called K-2. Many of these granite dishes were large and flat enough to accommodate a sleeping bag. Some were hidden away in the dark recesses of sheltering rocks, out of the wind, and some of these dark alcoves offered more than one flat place to sleep. I settled into one of these shelters with a camp mate. We fired up our Primus stove and made hot tea. Then we heated up a pot of bubbling, splattering instant mashed potatoes, cutting off chunks of cheddar cheese with a pocket knife and stirring them in. Everything to make a boy happy.

Early the next morning we climbed to the top of Capitol Peak via the airy Knife Edge. This sharp ridge drops off a thousand feet on either side. You just straddle it and scoot along. Our guide, Andy Carson, actually lived at the K-2 camp and escorted Outward Bound patrols to the top when they passed through. I was impressed. I thought, "This must be the life."

The Grand Alpine Expedition went on for another five days over invigorating terrain. There were wild mountain passes—Heckert Pass for example, hardly a pass at all, just a dent on an escarpment at 12,600 feet. We camped there, under a sheet of plastic tied to some rocks. When we woke in the morning, ice caked the inside of our "tent." I remember my tent-mate, Tom, leaning over a billycan of pancake batter, exhaling clouds of condensation as he stirred. Sometimes his postnasal drip fell into the mixture, but being hungry, I ate those flapjacks anyway.

One day our patrol was hiking up East Maroon Creek, a long valley with steep, ragged ridges on either side. Halfway along we just stopped and climbed straight up one of the ridges three thousand feet, then down the same distance on the other side to Conundrum Creek. We rewarded ourselves with a soak in Conundrum Hot Spring, just upstream. After another long day of backpacking, the expedition concluded with a six-mile run from Lead King Basin back to Marble.

All the patrols participated. I made it in forty-five minutes in the middle of the pack.

A letter awaited me from Dad. Everything was OK at home; he had some painting work; he hoped I was getting my scrawny muscles built up. Well, I still didn't have much body mass; it would be a long time before my forearms were as brawny as Dad's, but I definitely felt tougher.

With everybody back in camp we had a hootenanny. The patrols took turns singing made-up songs. We feasted on home-style cooking and drank glass after glass of wonderful cold milk. In the morning all the students would embark in small groups on a mapped-out three-day final expedition without our instructors. I was eager to get to bed. Instead, the staff kept us up with an interminable slide show about the K2 expedition. Then, about two in the morning we were rousted out of the sack to extinguish a practice "forest fire" – a jumble of logs in a clearing which had been doused with kerosene and set ablaze. "Remember, it's not out till every ember is cold."

Early in the morning we set out, two patrol mates and I, into unknown country. Tom and Dave had tented with me on the Grand Expedition, so we already had the wrinkles ironed out. We traveled swiftly over Anthracite Pass, down North Anthracite Creek and into Dark Canyon the first night. The second day we got behind schedule stumbling up the trackless Middle Anthracite and ended up sleeping in a jumble of jagged rocks on the side of Purple Mountain. I remember the intense joy I felt building a shelter that night. There is something deeply satisfying to me about stacking stones. The old stone savage in me, I guess.

We woke cold and achy. The route mapped for us prescribed an ascent of Purple Mountain as well as a string of summits eleven miles to the north. It wasn't feasible. We chucked the plan and headed back toward school, angling across boulder fields and descending wooded valleys till we intersected with the nearest jeep road. We got back to Outward Bound headquarters in mid-afternoon, which didn't impress our debriefing instructor. At least we didn't get royally chewed out like some fellows. One guy came out of the instructors' office sobbing.

We slept a long sleep in our shepherds' tents. Next day we laundered our clothes and checked in our gear. I wrote a thank you letter to Gates Rubber. We gathered for the last time around the campfire that evening, five patrols of hardy, mountain-savvy lads, and Joe Nold warmly congratulated us for completing the course. Then he awarded each of us a "man badge"—a Colorado Outward Bound patch embroidered with a compass and the school motto, "To serve, to strive, and not to yield." We felt we had earned it.

Senior in High School

1964-65

SCHOOL STARTED soon after I got home from Outward Bound. I belonged to a clique of misfits at Mapleton High in north Denver. The tallest, shortest, fattest, nerdiest kids belonged to our group. We spoke our own esoteric language called "Sayer," which we had invented in the eighth grade.

My buddies called me Stome (short for Stome-lah). The heavyset kid was Lumadenna (Aluminum Dennis). We mocked each other. We had our own club, the Rocky Mountain Gumbeaters' Society; our own finger-snapping, cud-chewing march; our own "conjugation": stis stese stose stem stay stat stooze; and our own versions of hit songs, such as this parody of Big Bad John: "Every day at the mine about a quarter to six, he compayed swow and they all said 'Stis!' Kind of tahnny at the shoulders, at the hips kind of doah, and you was a fooditzah to say you moah to Big Dotz."

We thought it was cool stuff.

I took a creative writing class in which logical exposition, not perverse double-talk, was upheld as the standard for acceptable writing. Mr. Metz expected more than twaddle. An early assignment required some paragraphs and revision. Here's my first paragraph:

> I'm dull sitting here in my desk, fat full of food and writing like a hypnotized block of wood. My clay brain utters nonsense, my mouth dribbles idiot cliches.

The revision:

> Sitting at my desk after lunch, I feel lethargic and bloated. I am in Creative Writing Class, but my mind is still in the cafeteria. I yawn and write a nonsensical paragraph. Oh well, I think, as I read the silly thing. I am still sleepy and unconcerned.

Second paragraph:

> What a funny looking intellectual! He undulates lazily past my chair like a fat eel slobbering at the mouth. He mumbles little nonessential slogans like, "Sure ho fer the world," and "How inna heck can I wash ma neck," "Man alive in 65." He's kinda hard to figure out. I'm not going to try, at least not this afternoon.

Revision:

> The boy ambles lazily past my desk as the bell rings
> to end the lunch period. He stares at his feet and
> his hands are limp at his sides. As I look up and
> smile at him, he mumbles. He seems to be walking
> in his sleep.

Mr. Metz's response:

> I am disappointed to say the least! This certainly
> shouldn't represent four full days of work on
> your part – rather it represents a few moments of
> sketchy thought without concern for the aims of
> the assignment. If this attitude persists, you will
> not do well in this class.

> GRADE D –

He had a point. I don't remember putting much effort into high
school. Yet it was a heady time for me. I read a lot—Kerouac novels,
absurdist plays, classics, Beat poets. My buddies and I were always
hashing things over—society, politics, religion, sex. We hung out at
the Capri restaurant drinking coffee—10 cents a cup with free refills—
talking tieb-talk and "philosophy" till one in the morning. Was the
cosmos an accident? Did it have a purpose? Syllogisms, taught to us by
Mr. Metz, led to a conundrum I had never before considered: if every
statement must be supported by two premises, how can the premises

in turn be supported, except by additional premises which must also be supported? My propositional world was dissolving in mid-air. And then the really big question: how do you get a girl to like you?

My buddy Rodney was a magician who could make cards and coins disappear while engaging you with clever patter. One afternoon we were racing around Denver in his low-slung Porsche when the highway patrol pulled us over. Rodney held out his driver's license, but when the patrolman reached for it—presto—it vanished. Then it rematerialized. I thought this was pushing things far enough, but Rodney remonstrated with the officer until he had talked him out of the ticket. Zippa de doo, just like that.

Then we drove to Smiley's place down by the stockyards. It was a rundown house but warm inside, dense with the aroma of chili. "Mom's is the best around," beamed Smiley as his mother ladled each of us a bowl of larruping chili so spicy it made our eyes water. I scarfed it down and asked for seconds.

One of Smiley's eyebrows was scarred from a fight. He'd gotten his head kicked a few times. He was a good-looker, hair slicked back in a ducktail. Some girl had promised to date him steady if he went Sosh, so he was thinking it over. "After all, I'm a lover, not a fighter," Smiley mused. Soshes combed their hair like the Beach Boys—dry with bangs. It was the new look.

The three of us hopped in Rodney's red speedster and headed north, the evening still young. I rapped a drum tattoo on the dashboard while Smiley talked about his latest romance. Rod said, "Wait a second, listen to that beat—it's cool." It was a percussion solo from the Ventures, a hectic rhythm I'd been practicing for weeks. I loved the twang of the guitar, the throbbing beat—a chemical yes. I would be a drummer someday. The girls would go crazy; they'd tear their hair out and chase me across the stage.

Talk turned to politics as we zoomed north on Washington, heading for Thornton, our home turf. My family had lived there for the last five years. Dad was still a housepainter, Mom a clerk in a department store. We were as working class as they come, and staunchly Republican. "You know Goldwater is going to lose," Smiley chided. To me this was irrelevant. You're right or you're wrong; that's what matters. I'd read *None Dare Call It Treason* and other conservative books that warned of America's slide to the left.

"Goldwater wants to blow the world to bits," he said. The week before, a political ad had appeared on TV: the freckle-faced girl counting daisy petals, the atom bomb.

"C'mon, you don't believe that."

"The guy's a warmonger." Goldwater had been caricatured in the media as a hare-brained idiot, as some kind of monster who wanted to put strontium 90 in our ice cream.

"Where's the evidence? I think you've been brainwashed." Smiley had drawn a cartoon for the school paper showing Goldwater in a leaky boat with LBJ triumphantly rowing by. My own efforts at political art lampooned Johnson's TV ads.

Rod swerved onto 58th, leaving the dark truck farms behind, and surged toward the streaming lights of the Valley Highway. "I love the

way this car handles," he said, gleaming and raising his bushy eyebrows. He dropped down a gear and stepped hard on the accelerator, the red speedster swooping obediently around the access ramp, the G's tugging at us, grins sliding across our faces.

Rod was a fan of the great race-car driver Juan-Manuel Fangio. Once, Rod told us, a car swerved in front of Fangio on the race track. The maestro double-clutched lightning fast and went right over the top of the oncoming car. We thrived on stories like that. Our heroes were cool, quick-witted.

We pulled into our favorite hangout, the Capri Motor Hotel and Restaurant in Thornton, where we scooted into a booth and ordered coffee. There weren't any teenagers, just a scattering of adults indulging in quiet conversation. Clinking glasses. Muzak in the background. Rod wanted to discuss an upcoming gig at the Paramount Theater, which would be hosted by KIMN radio, Denver's prominent rock station in those days. His friend, Bruce Spangler, was collaborating with the radio station on a Halloween magic show. Bruce had earned a national reputation for his needle-in-the-arm trick and was president of the Denver chapter of the Brotherhood of Magicians.

Our part in the gig: at a predetermined moment in the magic show all the lights would go out, and under cover of darkness, Rodney and friends would stand up and pelt the audience with wet spaghetti strands and pipe-cleaner spiders. Spangler would pay us ten bucks each. Only one wrinkle: gangs would be there from all over Denver, looking for trouble. At last year's Halloween event a magician had been stabbed. We talked it over. Smiley had a date that weekend, but I said I'd go. It was a chance to make some money.

I'd been saving lunch money to buy climbing hardware. Ten bucks in one night would quickly beef up my climbing rack.

A week after our meeting at the Capri, Rodney and I showed up at the Paramount. The marquee announced in bold letters "KIMN FREE SHOW TONIGHT." I felt puny walking through the big glass doors into a lobby full of tough-looking street kids. Mr. Clean was supposed

66

to be there that night. He'd be easy to spot: a tall, muscular black guy with a bald-shaven head and gold earring, a widely feared gang leader. His gang already knew the program from last year. When the lights went out, they may try to stab us. Rod disappeared into the crowd. I drifted down the left aisle and eased into one of the plush seats, trying to look inconspicuous. I had a plastic baggie full of wet spaghetti under my coat, and a pocketful of fuzzy spiders.

I was so terrified, I don't remember any of the magic performances. I was frozen to my seat, wondering if anybody suspected me. Then the lights went off. I stood up and furtively tossed a few spaghetti strands and pipe cleaner thingamajigs into the crowd and quickly sat back down. Dim aisle lights cast a soft glow on pant legs patrolling up and down the theater—hoods on the prowl looking for twerps like me. Was that Mr. Clean striding up the aisle? I scrunched lower in my seat. Was that the glint of his switchblade?

On the other side of the theater, Rodney got routed from his seat, chased out into the lobby, then up a flight of stairs to the balcony level, where he gave them the slip by locking himself in the manager's office, leaving the hoods to pace the hall on the other side of the door. An escape worthy of my friend, who counted Fangio and the great Houdini among his heroes. Finally the crowd went home. Bruce the master magician paid us our ten bucks each and we never saw Mr. Clean.

The day before the Paramount escapade, I had participated in a school-sponsored debate. The gymnasium with its polished floor and reverberant acoustics was set up with two long tables and a podium. I sat scrawling last-minute notes while seven hundred kids swarmed onto the bleachers to hear the Goldwater and Johnson factions duke it out five days before the national election. Joining me on the conservative team were some egghead-types with horn-rimmed glasses.

Anchoring the liberal team was the notorious Frank Prescott, a bowlegged, red-faced contrarian who never got anything but A's in high school. Once at a school assembly he stood up and cheered right in the middle of the principal's speech, just to prove that the students would mindlessly follow suit. Sure enough, he had them all on their feet, cheering who knows what.

Since Frank and I were both tieb-talkers, we could have conducted the whole debate in Sayer (make 'em doe or say fugede to Vietnam), but the student body wouldn't have appreciated it.

I sat fidgeting at the conservative table, tense as a greyhound. Mr. Joseph, the principal, introduced the contenders, and fur began to fly. "The world looks to America for sane leadership." Frank's voice echoed throughout the gymnasium. "Lyndon Johnson is the right man to lead America in these perilous times. We don't need a trigger-happy extremist at the helm."

"China has just detonated its first atomic bomb," our side countered, "and now we're going to reelect a man who's soft on Communism?" So the argument went, back and forth. When my turn came, I gripped the podium with sweaty palms and attacked the Democrats for accommodating Communist expansion. "In Vietnam our enemy is free to attack and retreat, while we run from one ambushed village to the next. American soldiers die without the promise of victory. We have to alter our strategy if we want to win. We must give our armed forces in Vietnam all the military and diplomatic support we have at our disposal. We must interdict the neutral supply lines which feed Communist military aggression in Vietnam.

"You already know that the Reds dominate a billion people. Senator Goldwater believes one thing that most of us have been taught not to believe: that Communism and capitalism are fighting to the death. There's no truth to the lullaby they sing nowadays, that Communism is just a harmless philosophy. We can't expect Red dictators to abandon a scheme of world domination they've pursued brutally and effectively for fifty years."

When the debate was over, the combatants from both sides resumed friendships as smoothly as if nothing had happened. Goldwater was soundly clobbered five days later, as Smiley predicted.

Mapleton chafed me. I bristled back in Sayer language. Motman, make me fooditz. Sometimes I wore two plaid shirts, one over the other, a signal—though it's doubtful anyone noticed—that I was a man of layered personality.

At home I brewed sake in the kitchen. I captured spiders, dipped them in hot paraffin and lifted them out to cool and rigidify—they looked so realistic. I phoned esoteric messages to KIMN Radio which they recorded and broadcast. I drew a portrait of myself as a sour-faced old man, and wrote cynical plays which my pals relished as gems of literature. Here's a scene from one:

> Setting—The front seat of a flashy sports car in the desert.
>
> Emily—You know, Lassie, I . . . I've been throwing this problem of personal intraflection for a few years—ever since I can remember—you know what I mean?
>
> Tod—(Drunkenly) Well, just remember that every kid's got to grow a beard. Just like in life.
>
> Emily—(She gives him a knowing smile.) Of course, Tod. You know, those beards can entangle a man hopelessly in the craggy branches of unrealization.
>
> Tod—(Sagely) Baby, I'll ask you for the rest, if you ever stop knowing and then knowing.
>
> Emily—(Emotionally caressing his shoulders) Oh, Tod!
>
> (A gila monster threatens to devour the car.)

I'm alone in the silent field. A wide, flat expanse with cottonwoods in the distance. I'm walking home through weeds to avoid the crowded bus. Burchfield leaned over and blew his fake snot down the back of my neck, and now I've had enough of the bus and everybody on it.

This school gets to me. The guys are bullies. The girls are remote. So walking home suits me just fine. There's something soothing about the open sky. I've walked a couple of miles up Washington Street from Mapleton High School—square, squat learning factory built of caramel-colored bricks. It's another mile and a half cutting across fields to my house—itself a squat, brick box—in the subdivision on the horizon. Dad struggles to make mortgage payments. More than once we've been to the brink of foreclosure.

I have a long stride. I'm singing and singing as I walk along—folk tunes and bits of melody—breaking brittle stems as I stride. And I am thinking about love—all steamed up about love. I've been reading Erich Fromm's *The Art of Loving*. He says falling in love is an explosive experience. Barriers between strangers suddenly collapse. I like the sound of that. May I please experience it soon?

There's a tall, sandy-haired girl in the junior class with that indefinable something I'm looking for, and her name is Anne-Marie Lukacz. She's austere, upright, motherly. Looking at her, you might say she's average. But I see a paleness, a sturdiness, a solidity, a softness, a fragility. When did she first catch my eye?

71

Fromm says that in erotic love there is a "craving for complete fusion." That speaks to the cauldron in my body. I want complete fusion—the blinding heat of an arc-welder's torch. I want to live and die for someone. Someone named Anne-Marie. So flesh-and-bone pure beautiful.

I follow the dusty road that wanders hit-and-miss through this stretch of field—the last patch of prairie between Denver and the widening suburbs. My feet pad softly. If I had my ocarina with me, I'd take it out of my pocket right now—reliable friend—and play a smooth, whistling song about Anne-Marie. What breeze blew her across my field of vision?

Out here away from everybody I sit in the dry weeds—a perfect place for thinking about the collective unconscious, dissolving syllogisms, and my biological destiny—for singing a song full of the grandeur of life. Heart's book, you are open now. I'm in love.

Open your eyes to me, sweet Anne-Marie. Your eyes are lambs. Your feet are tangled roots burrowing into the ground. I'm alone in this field of stubble, in this dry-leafed autumn, longing to come to you. Dare I tell you these things? Let's make farmloads of whoopee. I'll be your slide trombone; you be my homemade candy. I'll be your tomahawk; you be my pink motel.

I've never conversed with her. We're in none of the same classes, no friends in common. I doubt she knows my name. But that's part of the appeal—her complete inaccessibility. It fits right in with my meditations on nothingness.

I walk the rest of the way home. My parents are still at work. I make supper, macaroni and cheese, a frequent meal around this house. I boil the noodles, add condensed milk and big chunks of government cheese, salt and pepper. Yum, this is good stuff. I make plenty for everybody—Mom, Dad, brother, sisters.

The radio is cranked up while I cook. Blast-it-out rock and roll. I bounce around the kitchen. Radio has been a steady companion since seventh grade. I know the songs by heart. The guys on the radio make it sound so easy, this love thing. Every Joe so-and-so's got one girlfriend on his arm and two more gals waiting. And me, nothing but aching emptiness in the air

It gripes me that the guys at school have such a low opinion of girls. They brag about their exploits. Spell out the nasty details to each other. For them it's all so easy. To them, girls are nothing but garbage. Anne-Marie, I will treat you with respect. I'll wring my heart out for you till it's a dry rag. Go panting to my death.

Why are girls attracted to bullies? Why did they huddle in a tight circle last week at the cafeteria door, watching one of the big shots at school rough up a Japanese kid, clouting him on the head, kneeing him, shoving him, banging his lip? Such a tight knot of girls. Like a welt, so intensely focused. Their dander was up—they wanted blood.

I keep thinking about Erich Fromm's different kinds of love: love for family, love for friends, love for humanity, love for pure being. Fromm speaks of people who sit cross-legged for days and years, emptying themselves, thinking of nothing at all, until they achieve oneness with the universe. I have tried, so far without success, to clear my mind of all things. I keep staring at the walls of my bedroom, waiting for them to dissolve. I feel like an alien floating in the Black Sea. I tell Dad that nothing matters, which gets him really agitated.

I'm sprawled on my bed, where I spend a miserable lot of time. The radio is playing "My Girl"—sweet, tormenting song. My pillow feels like a bag of cement. I thrash around. There must be a girl out there somewhere for me. I groan, roll up against the cold, bare wall. Where is she, Lord?

One day after school in late fall I walked north on Washington Street, lost in lonely thought. At the place where the street passed an open field, I stepped over a beat-down fence and noticed a length of rope lying in the grass. I picked it up and numbly fixed my eyes on a cottonwood silhouetted in the distance. I don't know how serious I was, but there was at least a dim thought of ending it all as I walked, rope in hand, through the stubble toward that tree. Part-way there I heard someone call my name. I turned back toward Washington Street.

It was Anne-Marie.

She was standing beside an open car door, waiting for me. She and her friend Skip offered me a lift home. The three of us chatted like old friends all the way there. A few weeks later I got up my courage and asked her for a date. I was a senior in high school, and this would be my first date—ever. Before this intensely romantic fling drew to a conclusion, we would go on a total of two.

The first date presented a challenge, since I barely knew how to drive, but Mom came to the rescue. She coached me up and down I-25— Denver's Valley Highway—till she had me confidently swerving and weaving in full-speed commuter traffic while she sat on the passenger side, emotionless as a combat general.

When the big night rolled around I chauffeured Anne-Marie to the heart of Denver, to the very hip Analyst Coffeehouse on a dark street where vagrants and cognoscenti congregated. It was a wacky, crooked little establishment, dimly lit, with a few creaky wooden tables. A venerable espresso machine occupied the back counter. The menu featured, among other things, squashed peanut butter and jelly sandwiches for a dollar and a half, pricey in those days. A guy who could've passed for a sawmill hand or a Communist insurgent slouched on a stool, understood to be the "stage." A single light shone on him

75

as he worked his guitar and sang in a gold-edged voice about the wandering life.

Our attempts at conversation were awkward. She was restrained but courteous. Mainly we worked on our food and sat through Bogie's *Petrified Forest* projected on the coffeehouse wall in flickering black-and-white. The story was over our heads—about a writer and a gangster. Male egos clashing at a lonely truck stop.

Our second date took us to Cherry Creek High for a screening of Gaston Rebuffat's *Entre Terre et Ciel*, complete with a personal appearance by the famous mountaineer. But Anne-Marie wasn't interested in mountains. Our conversation in the car centered around a guy she was dating who wanted to start a "Sosh band." Everything would be Sosh—hair, pants, shoes. At evening's end I dutifully escorted her to her front door. A kiss was out of the question.

For some incomprehensible reason, the powers at Mapleton High granted the Gumbeaters permission to organize and present a school assembly. It was to be a magic show and, as we envisioned it, an extravaganza—an amusing and amazing display of idiosyncratic talent. We would wow 'em. Ladies and gents—For some reason it all worked according to plan, though we hadn't rehearsed. First, we shuffled across the stage snapping our fingers and chewing our cuds: Rodney the magician; Frank, the red-faced genius; Lumadenna (who taught me to play pinochle); Greg (who would later hold a gun on me in a bunkhouse in Wyoming—it was my own fault for losing my temper and throwing hay hooks at him); Vick with goggle glasses (whom Rodney hypnotized and suspended between two chairs); Mike Valentine, the tallest kid in school (who disappeared into military intelligence during the Vietnam War—no one has seen him since); Smiley, tough, debonair; Johanna, a nice Jewish girl who hung out with the Gumbeaters (the only girl who would dance with me—we did a rubbery rendition of "I Feel Fine"). Eggheads, motmen, misfits, chess players, coin collectors, all chewing cud in unison, a bovine chorus line. We were a slovenly bunch, exhibiting ourselves like so much beef on the hoof.

Out in the auditorium sat all the girls I'd had crushes on for the past five years, going back to junior high; not to mention the head boy and head girl, cheerleaders, basketball stars, wrestling champs, strumpets and Casanovas, dance royalty and pugilists. For once they had to pay attention to us.

No sooner had the chorus line shuffled offstage than Greg reappeared on the left, tugging a rope. He dug in his heels like a bulldogging buckaroo. The rope strained and quivered. He puffed his cheeks under the exertion, slowly backing across the stage. Then, what do you know! Here came the same Greg from the opposite end, resisting as he was pulled across.

Next, Rodney and I worked our magic, tossing invisible golf balls back and forth to one another across the stage. We had our own background music—the Nairobi Trio—and had appeared professionally at the Wilshire Country Club. Golf balls appeared, disappeared, multiplied. It amazed me even though I knew the trick.

Time for my zombie routine. See? Nothing in my hands but this flimsy silk kerchief. Now—whoa! It rises into the air, wobbles, takes on a life of its own, bobs up and down. Mysterious whatever-it-is, hovering over the crowd. I bow to everyone, including the lovely Anne-Marie, herself afloat somewhere in that sea of faces, and show that there is nothing under the silk, nothing at all.

Next, Rode-nah the Magnificent commanded center stage with his professional fire-eating act, blowing fantastic fire shapes into the atmosphere—pulsating balls of fire exploding and melting; golden, whirling, bright-plumed wisps of cotton candy. Rodney—flawless entertainer—dramatically waving his arms, describing golden arcs, spewing liquid jets of flame from his mouth. Blasts of scorching heat. Halos, afterimages. All against the black cavity of the auditorium.

We had lassoed Frank, unfit as he was, into starring in the final act of our program. The classic, the unforgettable sawing-the-woman-in-half routine, featuring our own inimitable Frank, impresario of klutziness. Give him a little liberty and watch what happens. "First, some flowers for the lady," he muttered. Lifting his coat flap to reveal the hook apparatus underneath, he produced an artificial bouquet and handed it to Johanna. "Voila." Next came a silk handkerchief and a completely uncalled-for reference to the "sneaky peek" elastic device up his sleeve. Next Johanna climbed into a wooden box stretched across two sawhorses. As soon as Frank started to saw, she shrieked and ran offstage.

Thus our great show came to an end.

The moment finally arrived in late May when the class of '65—boys in black robes, girls in white (we were the imps; they were the angels)—filed into the crowded Mapleton gymnasium to receive our diplomas. Frank gave a rough-hewn valedictorian speech, his red face glowing under his mortar board, and managed to mispronounce the superintendent's name in the process. Parents watched anxiously. The glee club sang "Moon River." There were lots of tears and hugs, for which I had little use. Dad and I almost got in a fight afterward. It was the only time in my life I wanted to haul off and slug him.

After the ceremony, some buddies and I were parked on the tarmac in front of Mapleton High School, ready to make our getaway. Rod was in the driver's seat; I sat on the passenger side. From the crowd of leave-takers emerged Miss Thatcher—youngest teacher on the faculty, in her late twenties, with bobbed blonde hair and a sheath dress. She wandered over to us, deftly knelt by my open car window, leaned in, and lit her cigarette on mine. She took a draw, let it drift into her brain and exhaled a sigh of relief. She joked a bit, wished us well, like a demoiselle bidding adieu to a crew of pirates. We were leaving harbor—pushing off into the unknown.

Elephant Buttress

1966

BY THE TIME I was a sophomore at the University of Colorado in Boulder, I had become a real aficionado of rocks. I had gazed down at the Navajo desert from the summit of Shiprock and scampered up the perfect basalt columns of the Devil's Tower. I wrote poetry and wandered barefoot around campus, always dreaming of my next vertical encounter.

One warm fall morning in 1966, my roommate, Frank Prescott, and I decided to ditch classes and go climbing. We hopped on his red Kawasaki and roared out of town. We belted out rock songs as we leaned into the curves, heading for Boulder Canyon in the foothills.

Ten minutes later we stopped in the shadow of four cliffs known as the Elephant Buttresses. We jumped off the bike and stared up. The name fit. I could easily imagine the rock formations as a row of gargantuan gray elephants. "How about the Fourth Buttress?" Frank asked, pointing to the cliff farthest to the south. "The northwest face looks perfect." That morning I was full of bravado, ready to take on any challenge. "You've got it," I agreed.

Strapping on my rucksack, I followed Frank as he headed for the creek at the foot of the cliffs. We took off our lug-soled kletterschuhes and waded across. On the other side we relaced them and scrambled through the brush to the base of the Fourth Buttress.

Frank tossed me one end of a 120-foot Goldline nylon rope. We knotted the rope around our waists. I took the lead on the first pitch. Frank paid out the rope from below, ready to cinch it off if I slipped. Once I got to a ledge about a hundred feet up he'd join me. Then we would switch positions for the next pitch.

I started climbing the perpendicular wall of rock, reveling in the hard, ripply feel of the cold stone. Groping for a good hold, I jammed my fingertips into a fissure above my head. Then I wedged the tip of one shoe into the same crevice, drew my other foot up, slotted it, and pushed up to an even higher hold. Like a spider, I slowly worked my way up the face of the cliff. Feeling cocky, I stopped only once to hammer in a piton and clip my line through it. If I slipped, it would shorten the distance of my fall.

At last I reached the ledge and hoisted myself onto it. I rested a moment and breathed in the crisp, clean air. *This sure beats being stuck in some stuffy classroom*, I thought. "On belay!" I shouted down. Frank's voice drifted up, "Climbing!" I began taking in rope as he climbed toward me.

My friend clambered onto the ledge and gave me a high five. In a burst of joy we boomed out Stevie Wonder's "Uptight (Everything's Alright)." We were on top of the world.

Frank looked up at the steep cliff above us. "Okay," he said, "my turn." He disappeared around the corner of the ledge, the rope trailing after him. The scrape of his shoes against the granite faded as he climbed higher. I sat on the ledge, legs dangling over the precipice, in position to secure Frank if necessary. But the end of the rope lay in a pile beside me. I hadn't bothered to anchor in. As I waited for my friend to reach the top, about fifty feet up, I watched swallows wheel and swoop, and caught a refreshing whiff of pine in the canyon breeze. The creek we'd crossed was now just a slate-green ribbon below.

Frank's got to be thirty feet up by now, I thought, when suddenly I felt an overpowering presence beside me. I turned to see a blindingly radiant man standing on the ledge. He was over seven feet tall, in a robe of lightning white. His voice penetrated me with authoritative clarity: "Anchor in now, or you're a dead man!"

I looked around frantically. My eyes fell on a jutting block of granite to my right. I had just wrapped my end of the rope around it twice when a dark shape plummeted past me. Frank had lost his hold. He'd fallen off the cliff. Before I could brace myself and take in the rope to secure him, I was yanked off the ledge by his weight. In the next second, I jerked roughly to a halt. The rope dug painfully into my side.

"Frank, you okay?" I called, afraid I wouldn't hear an answer. I'd only slid off the ledge. Frank had plunged sixty feet. After what seemed a long while, I made out a faint "Yeah." Slowly he climbed up to me with none of his usual boisterous enthusiasm. His ruddy face had gone ghostly. Neither of us felt like talking.

When we got back on the ledge, the angel was gone. Frank and I took the easiest route to the top, deeply shaken. In silence we walked down the other side of the Elephant Buttress, picking our way through the boulders. "Man," Frank said finally, as we packed our gear on his bike, "good thing you anchored in."

Deliverance

1970

I HAD A LOT of screwy ideas. That, for example, as a cat I had prowled the back alleys of Babylon in a previous life. Worse than that, I thought I was God. That somehow I had broken through the taboo against knowing who you are—the one that keeps you from realizing your "godhood." I had seen the great white light, and it was me.

By this time I had a wife and baby daughter, both of whom I loved dearly, but was in no condition to properly care for, mesmerized as I was by psychedelic drugs and rock climbing. We had an apartment on Pine Street in Boulder. I rode my bike to work every day at the brickyards, since we didn't own a car.

The brick factory was a hip place. Some climbers worked there and quite a few stoneheads. I remember opening up a tinfoil package of hashish and passing it around at lunch break. The stuff looked like tarry brown sugar. We ate it and went back to work in the molding room, where clay was continuously extruded onto a tray, sliced with wires, and sent down a conveyor belt, where we pulled the wet, steaming bricks off and stacked them on pallets for transfer to the kilns. We thought we were intensely clever and creative as we swiped up excess mud off the conveyor belt and flung it at the walls, the mud making inexpressibly exotic designs, ludicrous mud-glob forms that taunted and tantalized.

Sometimes we worked outside stacking bricks on the carousel. We wore our rubber-coated gloves to shreds on the freshly fired bricks. Red, the foreman, stood there urging us to stack faster or we'd be replaced by a machine. Once, a load of bricks collapsed and knocked me to the ground. When I came to, Red was standing over me, hands on his hips, telling me to get back to work. We decided that when the crusty old guy died, they would just bake him in a kiln and turn him into a brick.

But we were fond of him. One particularly fine day when our climbing juices were flowing, he allowed us to take the afternoon off so we could clamber on the cliffs above Boulder. "I know what those days were like," he said.

I did some guiding. One of my clients was Dick Balkins, a genial fellow with apple cheeks and bald forehead, an anesthesiologist who had climbed some routes with me in the canyons around Boulder. We became friends. He and his wife, Dottie, adopted me and Dorene and our baby daughter. They had us to their home for vegetarian meals, gave us gentle instruction in baby care, took us to church. They were Seventh-Day Adventists. Sometimes Dick came to our apartment on what were essentially pastoral visits. Once, he found me sitting cross-legged on the floor separating seeds out of a big wooden bowl of marijuana. He didn't blink an eyelash.

"Let's study the Bible," he said, unfolding a collapsible reading stand and setting it on the floor in front of the mattress that served as our living room couch. Dorene and I sat together on the mattress while Dick read us a lesson. We had worksheets to fill out, the answers to be found in the pages of scripture on the stand in front of us. Dick's scriptural knowledge was impressive. It dawned on me that although I had a Christian upbringing I really didn't know much of the Bible. A ray of sun was quietly shining into our lives.

On a cold morning in late December 1969, I joined Jim Erickson and John Behrens to climb a new route in Eldorado Canyon. John was stocky with a round, benign face, sandy hair, dimpled chin—girls would call him a teddy bear. Jim Erickson had a gentleman's bearing and dark curly hair. He was a preeminent figure in Colorado rock climbing in those days. The new route was his idea. It would take us up the precipitous west wall of the Bastille, a 400-foot stone tower at the entrance to Eldorado Canyon. This would be a fresh line up the Bastille, tackling a section that had not been climbed before.

John Behrens took the first lead. He breezed up it, smoothly maneuvering his way on small but adequate holds. I took delight in watching his upward progress, the liquid folding and unfolding of his body, an elegy to being there. Jim followed; then my turn came. I remember delicious moves up a steep, conglomerate face, gray-purple pebbles for fingerholds, creases and edges appearing at the proper moment, bridging across delicate footholds, then clambering onto a platform to join the other two. We were already halfway up the Bastille. A chill wind bit into us, and I started shivering. John kindly lent me a bulky sweater, hand-knit by his wife. It was a work of art, cream and ivory-colored. I pulled it on and felt the warmth flow back into my arms and torso.

Jim Erickson asked, "Would either of you like to take the next lead?" The rust-red rock above our heads was slightly overhanging with rotten little fingers dangling down. I had no inclination to tackle it. John told him, "This is your route. You should have the honor." Jim engaged the rock with craftsman's skill, moving over a difficult bulge and up another hundred feet to the top. John followed without incident. Again I was last on the rope.

Out on the wall I quickly sensed the desperation of the moves Erickson had so efficiently dispatched. Here goes. Pulling hard on the rotten little upside-down fingers, I strained upward, then came to a tugging halt. Looking down I saw John's cream-colored sweater snagged on a protuberance at my waist. I had no choice but to lunge with all my might, tearing a sizable hole in it.

The rest of the climb went easy. We congratulated each other at the top and named the route Hair City. I handed John the torn sweater, hoping his wife would somehow understand. The route has become a classic in Eldorado. The cold sky and steep rock are still tangible in my book of memories.

Dorene and I now lived in a Victorian house in an old arboreal neighborhood in downtown Boulder. Our second-floor apartment was clean, spartan. There were a few occult and psychedelic items strewn around: a *Zap* comic book, the latest Beatles albums, a deck of tarot cards, my oversize lingam and yoni painting. Weird literature on the bookshelf: Edgar Cayce, Carlos Castaneda, R.D. Laing, Lobsang Rampa, and Richard Fariña, whose *Been Down So Long*, consisting largely of nonsequiturs, summed up my approach to life. We had a respectable bed and several white-draped windows gazing out onto the branches of tall maples and elms. We were about to be turned inside out.

In mid-January 1970, two weeks after the Bastille, a friend gave us some mescaline. We ingested it and were soon washed out to sea, anchors aweigh. The drug rendered my wife catatonic. I swam convulsively on the wooden floor of our apartment, flopping like a mackerel, mopping the floor with my body. A fine kettle of fish. La la. The room throbbed with orange light.

Our friend Harold accompanied us on this manic journey. Though he had taken the same drug, he didn't thrash on the floor, but sat unperturbed on the living room mattress with a whisper of a smile. He was known for this – quietly smiling while others were freaking out. That's why we called him Weird Harold. He would be an anchor for us in the unhinged hours that followed.

Melting swamp. Swirling madness. I see it now, he thinks, thinking he sees it now. A maiden in chains gazes upward, perishing in the flames of hell. The Moody Blues croon their anthem—just what the truth is they can't tell. The phone rings. The phone rings. The phone rings. The phone rings.

Baby Aimee senses the panic and starts crying. We can't get her to stop. Dorene is afraid to hold our little child because she might drop her. I search the telephone book for a doctor. My detached finger dials the number. "Hello? Our baby is crying. We don't know what to do." The doctor knows something fishy's going on. Meanwhile, Harold has picked up the baby, spoken softly to her, walked around the apartment patting her on the back. "I think we're okay now," I tell the doctor.

Dorene watches, terrified, as demons enter and exit her arms. They look like Thai wood carvings. The floor dissolves beneath her feet.

Intimate snow, rays of sunshine. It's all right, the Beatles tell us. They stride across the street, dressed in white, spokesmen for the sun. We float in an existential soup. From beyond these throbbing walls a malevolent power is poised to consume us. I stare at the wall, where Blake's tyger burns brightly. His mouth yawns open. His teeth are receding hallways, a succession of past lives.

Harold to the rescue, freshening the apartment with Brubeck's new oratorio, "Light in the Wilderness." I was with the Father before the foundation of this world. Assuring words in the middle of chaos. My wife and I lie down on the big bed, exhausted by the overwhelming worlds washing over us. No more Captain Cosmo. There is something bigger than me. I definitely am not God.

A black imp appears at my bedside and will not go away. Nasty thing. I say to him impotently, "Jesus loves you." He looks queer when I say that—of course Jesus doesn't love him, but that's all I know to say. Dark trees outside our window are sagging like wax. The sublime consciousness begins to peel around the edges. The effects are wearing off.

In the course of this mescal-induced madness I have conceived that I owe a climbing acquaintance a karmic debt from some previous life. In the morning I pay him a visit. He comes out on his porch, slightly bemused, to talk to me, a buttery golden beam of light emanating from the center of his forehead. The next day we go climbing together in Boulder Canyon, and I notice that, instead of the beam of light, there is a swollen zit in the middle of his forehead.

I had been taking drugs for three years. Anything I could get my hands on. I loved to ride my magic carpet into the cosmic void. See auras around people. The eye coming up out of the abyss and all that. I had lots of clever insights and flipped-out revelations. I spent a few days in jail, but my parents hired a good lawyer to get me out—not that they could afford it. Mom was earnestly asking God to deliver me from bondage.

The bum trip stunned me. All my drug experiences up till then had been "good." Since high school days, I had sought the white, mysterious light, the blank screen Erich Fromm wrote about. Drugs pulled back the curtain and allowed me to see into another realm. I had no knowledge of the biblical injunction against sorcery. I sincerely thought I was getting close to God this way.

In the middle of January, a few days after the mescaline trip, Mom called to invite us to hear Harald Bredesen, a charismatic preacher visiting the Denver area. God had already gotten my attention. My resistance was demolished. So we went to the meeting, held in a handsome red brick Episcopal church in downtown Denver. A small group had gathered there, maybe 30 people.

Dorene and I sat near the front, with Mom and our baby daughter Aimee in the pew behind us. Bredesen caught me completely off-guard. I expected a fire-breathing blunderbuss. This gentle soul welcomed us with a boyish smile. He sported a clerical collar and radiant tan—he'd been hanging out with Pat Boone in California. He told of a recent adventure of Pat's in the recording world. Pat had been ready to sign with the same company that produced the album with John Lennon and Yoko Ono naked on the cover. This company planned to promote his next album with the catchy phrase, "Pat Boone sings his ass off." Harald urged him not to sign, and challenged him: "Are you willing to die to your career?"

Pat had recently received the baptism in the Holy Spirit. Now his commitment to Christ was being put to the test. He had repented of making questionable deals without praying first. Pat now sought God for wisdom. He told the record company he was a changed man and was no longer willing to compromise his faith. Surprisingly, they agreed to work with him anyway on his terms.

Harald Bredesen told this story to demonstrate God at work in a celebrity's life. He assured us that God could rescue us too. Then he asked a terrifying question. "What would you do if you got to the gates of heaven, and they wouldn't let you in?" It hit me between the eyes. Dorene was silent. In a panic I murmured, "Jesus." Years of occult confusion could not obliterate what I knew to be true, that Jesus is the door to eternal life. Harald led the small congregation in the sinner's prayer. Dorene and I asked God to forgive our sins for the sake of his Son, to indwell us and set us free.

Bredesen then stepped off the podium and seated himself on the carpeted steps at the front of the sanctuary, where he proceeded with a simple, nonthreatening talk about the gift of the Holy Spirit. "If you ask for bread, will the Father give you a stone? If you ask for a fish, will he give you a serpent?" He explained that Jesus was the baptizer— baptism simply meaning immersion. Jesus would immerse us in his wonderful Holy Spirit. Bredesen took the fear and hocus-pocus out of it.

Having been raised in Pentecostal churches, I had the idea that this was something you achieved after great travail—something reserved for super-Christians. I had wanted this gift since I was a boy, but always felt unworthy to receive it. That's why I had turned to drugs, because I hungered for intense spiritual experience.

At the end of his talk, Dorene and I went forward together and knelt at the front of the church. God came down and burst upon me in an ocean of light and glory. I don't know how to describe it. Maybe like a spiritual atom bomb or something, or standing under Niagara Falls. God overwhelmed me with his power and his joy. It was real and true and good, unlike anything I had experienced before.

I began to speak in tongues, praising God in a heavenly language. Jesus was filling me to overflowing with his love, his peace, his purity, his freedom. Then he showed me a demon that was ruling my life—a spirit of drugs wedged down into my being like a keystone in an arch. It weighed tons. It had been usurping my thoughts and ripping off my personality.

Here we were in this genteel Episcopal church. Drunk on the newfound power that God had just given me, I began yelling in tongues at the evil spirit, commanding him to come out of me. The heavy keystone lightened up and floated out the top of my head. It turned light as a feather and blew away. And it's never been back. I went from loving drugs—I could never get stoned enough—to having no use for them. Bang. In the snap of a finger, God delivered me.

In the midst of all this I started laughing. Miles of relief gushed out of me in deep-rolling bellylaughs. I laughed on and on, yelling as loud as I could and carrying on in an outrageous way. Meanwhile, Dorene knelt next to me, quietly praying in another language.

This was the watershed event in our lives. God graciously turned us right-side-out and set our feet on a new path.

Out West

1970-71

WE HAD JUST BEEN DELIVERED from the drug world and were setting off on a brand new life. We owned practically nothing. I had courted my wife, gotten married, and had a child—all with no car, just a bicycle. I biked to the brickyards every day and stacked bricks.

Dorene and I were excited about sharing our new Christian life with our hippy friends, but they weren't interested. Back at the apartment we tried to witness to Harold, the guy who had sat on the mattress totally stoned while somehow having it together. Dorene wanted to tell him what had happened to us, but there was a witch in our apartment who wanted to prevent Harold from hearing any of it. As Dorene started to climb out the window to Harold, who was sitting on the roof, the witch pulled her back in. She called to him through the window, "We've found Jesus."

I told Milo, my old roommate and fellow doper, "You've got to turn to Jesus." But he wanted nothing to do with him. Dorene and I decided: You know what? It's time to leave Boulder. Let's get out of this hippy world and try something else.

Dad gave me his beat-up old Ford to drive. So we hopped in this crazy paint wagon and headed west. We had our baby daughter, a box of cereal, a portable washing machine, and that was it.

We drove over Loveland Pass, up through the hairpins and snowdrifts. Halfway up the pass the little rod that connects the gas pedal fell off, and traffic started backing up all the way down the pass while I was under the car trying to wire it back together. Finally we got over the pass and on to Carbondale. I decided to show Dorene where I had attended Outward Bound, so we drove toward Marble. We slid around a curve near the Darien Ranch and went off into a snowdrift and couldn't get out. We saw some little cabins down there, buried in snow. An old cowpoke named Roy answered when we knocked on the ranch house door. He was bald as a billiard ball—he'd lost his hair in a mustard gas attack in World War I. He called the owners in town, and they gave us permission to stay in one of the cabins. Roy told us some great stories. One was about a cowboy he knew who had been shot in the butt with an Indian arrow. Roy didn't like going to town, so we'd pick up groceries for him once a week in the "big city" of Carbondale (population 1,500).

We stayed there a month. Cats snarled in the attic. I read the devotional books Mom sent along when we left Boulder. Having no Bible, I picked up a Jehovah's Witness version at the library, but it didn't sit right. One night as I walked under the stars a deep burden pushed me down to my knees. I felt an unbearable, bitter dread in the

97

core of my being. Not understanding what it could mean, I cried to God in an unknown language. What was God telling me?

We lived in that tiny cabin a month, then moved to the Crystal River Ranch on the plateau west of Carbondale, where I bucked bales and shoveled cow crap and pushed cows up and down and around. You work seven days a week on that deal and you work from sunup to sundown. I think they provided us with beef—you get all the beef you want to eat. There was another old-timer also named Roy, this one having spent most of his life as a lumberjack. He lived in a tucked-away cabin down in some arroyo on the Crystal River spread. He was a husky old boy with a florid face and round nose who liked to entertain us ranch hands with wild tales from his lumberjack days. One time he got pretty lively describing a fight he'd been in. "Then I picked this feller up and bonged his head like this." To demonstrate, Roy picked me up like a log and rammed my head into the back bumper of a pickup truck. Next thing you know I was flat on the ground. He'd only meant it as a love tap.

Roy preferred "buckskin" (venison) to beef. He dined on it every night. A salty old cowpoke, he talked to the cows in a raspy voice as we drove them along. Once I heard him mutter to a calf sprawled on the ground, "It's your misfortune and none of my own." I tried my hand at bossing the cows around: "Git up there! Heeyah!" The foreman, this rugged Red Ryder-looking guy, got disgusted with me for carrying on like that. He gave me orders to just drive the cattle down the trail and keep my mouth shut.

Chet Crowley, another of the hired hands, pastored the local Pentecostal church and served as town marshal. He'd done his time in Vietnam—led a platoon around the jungle and never lost a man. Chet was built like a bull and always had a wrinkly smile and sparks coming out of his eyes. He wanted to go back to Vietnam, but his wife wouldn't let him. He said, "I put my foot down to let her know who was boss, then she put her foot down right on top of mine."

The Crowleys were real nice people. We met them soon after we came to the valley. Chet's wife, Imelle, was a country lady with freckles and luxuriant red hair. Man, could she play the piano! The ranch gave me a few hours off each Sunday to go to church. We had some serious good times down there. When those people prayed, they prayed all at once, full blast. We sang like that too—lots of glorious songs about heaven and what a happy day that will be when we all go marching around the throne of God. Chet did a fine job of preaching. So that was a taste of the hereafter down there at the Pentecostal Holiness Church in Carbondale.

Some of our hippy friends from Boulder hopped on a freight train and came out to see us. They made a movie of their trip and sat right on the front row at church to get the full flavor of what had happened to us. One of them, my climbing partner Bill Stephens, was murdered a few years later at his apartment in Boulder. It may have been about a drug deal, or it may have been political, since Bill was trying to get several different activist groups merged onto one page. He and I talked lively politics, hitchhiked together, slept in a public outhouse, and made a movie with a strangely prescient scene of him messing with a tombstone in the same graveyard where he later was buried.

Later that spring I took photography classes at Colorado Mountain College, learned the gidgets and gadgets, f stops and focal lengths, stinky chemicals and silver halide crystals, and fancied myself capturing the quintessential moment like Henri Cartier Bresson. Then I got hired to teach a course at Oregon Outward Bound. We bought a pickup truck and drove out there. My wife stayed in a tent with Aimee, now a one-year-old starting to walk, while I shepherded a pack of teenage boys around the Oregon woods for a month, surrounded by red-barked madrones, rhododendrons, ferns, and waterfalls. We saw a moose up there dipping algae out of the water with his antlers. The boys and I climbed some fantastic obsidian cliffs, tromped up glaciers, and jumped deep blue crevasses.

One night before the course started, I got stuck on the side of a mountain with another instructor. We just had to sit our little fannies down on the ice all night long and shiver like crazy. During that week of instructor training were off having a great time in the woods and climbing our brains out. Then each of us was supposed to go out on solo. I don't particularly like sitting alone for three days and starving. I like my meals regular and on time. And I don't like the boredom of just sitting there. So I sneaked into camp, got together with my wife, and we conceived our second child while everybody else was out on solo.

We were fresh out of hippy world, and still had a back-to-earth mindset. *The Whole Earth Catalogue* and all that. I was coming off a lot of goofy ideas—reincarnation and a lot of crazy things. Once the Outward Bound course was over, we decided, well, let's go look up this commune we've heard about. It was out there on Rattlesnake Road near Eugene. It was everything you ever would want a commune to be. They had their own produce gardens, their own mechanic shop. They took turns going into town and preaching on the streets, while the other half of the community would be doing cottage industries: making candles and quilts, baking bread, canning, hiring themselves out as teams of carpenters.

We went to their worship service, and there we were with little Aimee. This really hip lady sat up front playing her acoustic guitar singing a song she had written herself, and Aimee started crying in the middle of it. They were disturbed to have a crying baby in their service. I thought, wait a minute—! They let us know it wasn't appreciated, and then they let us know they felt that God didn't really want us to be part of their commune.

Back in Boulder days, that had been our pipedream. Our little group of hippies seriously thought we were going to move to British Columbia and start a commune up there, so we were very oriented to the commune idea. Then we went to Oregon and saw a real one, but they said, "No, we don't want you."

On our way back to Colorado we stopped in Montana to see Dorene's folks. We tried to apologize to them for our errant lifestyle, including an unwedded pregnancy, but they didn't buy it. They were pretty skeptical of me. They figured, once a druggie always a druggie. It was hard to convince people I had changed.

Harold, from our Boulder days, also became a Christian. He moved to Alaska, built a primitive cabin at the base of Denali, and lived a hermit's life. He'd go out to civilization once in a while to buy a bag of coffee and a bag of beans. He was so isolated that one day he opened the door to his cabin and there was a wolf standing there looking him right in the eyes. They stared at each other for a long time. Finally the wolf turned and walked away. Eventually Harold moved to town and became an elder in the Orthodox Church in Alaska.

After we'd been back in Carbondale only a short time, I decided to go to Bible school. So we moved to Grand Junction, at the western edge of Colorado, where we lived in an attic apartment directly above the administrative offices of Intermountain Bible College. It was anti-Pentecostal: they didn't like all the excitement and fanaticism and miracles; they were too conservative for that. I was learning Greek and church history and having a great time.

At the same time, I worked across the street at Mesa College as a dishwasher and, of all the ridiculous things, a bouncer at the school cafeteria—I was just this scrawny-necked kid. The students there could get unruly, throwing food around the room and knocking over chairs. One time some footballers were hunched around a table in the cafeteria. One of them poured a puddle of lighter fluid on the table, stared at it awhile, then lit it on fire. I approached him and said, "You can't be doing this kind of stuff in here." He snarled, "If you touch me, I'll kill you." So I decided, well, I don't need this job that bad.

A lot of us students at Bible college were ex-hippies. We decided to start our own ministry, which is typical of kids that age—just grab the bull by the horns and go for it. So we rented a house and started a crash pad. Anybody who was down and out or bumming around on drugs could come and stay there. We'd have prayer meetings at night. Read the Bible, tell them our testimony, and sing songs.

Dorene and I attended two Pentecostal churches while we lived in Grand Junction: an old-fashioned one Sunday mornings and a wild, fiery one weekday nights. The regular, old-fashioned one took me back to my roots, like the church Dad pastored when I was a boy. The other one was off-the-cuff, not sanctioned by anybody. Pastor Slader and Brother Miracle were in charge. They would preach—man, they would get up there and preach, preach, preach. Then they'd call on people in the audience, "Now you come up here and preach." Slader had a big bass drum. Instead of shouting amen, he'd pound the drum while the other guy was preaching. They were praying for miracles; there was a lot of praying in tongues, a lot of prophesying, and a lot of fasting—people going for long periods of time without eating, and just . . . hyper-spiritual, extremely on the edge.

In the middle of all that, a lady evangelist showed up. She was a Jewish lady with dark eyebrows and a sharp little nose, and she preached this fiery sermon. At times she would scream and growl. It was an extraordinary performance, to put it mildly. The power of God was so strong that I leaped out of my chair and ran forward, hoping to dive headfirst into the glorious pool of light in the front of the room. I got about halfway up the aisle before God dropped me to my knees. Not so fast.

She announced, "God wants to open a Teenage Challenge in this Grand Junction area." And we're all, amen! amen! And, lo and behold, she had a son who was college age who was beyond backslidden; he was an open follower of Satan. So, sure she wanted a Teen Challenge there, because she was hoping somebody would reach out to her son. Then she made a general call to the whole congregation. "Who's going to witness to my son?" Since the kid belonged to a Satanist church, I stayed low, hoping it wasn't me who was supposed to go do that.

Over the next few days it began to eat on my conscience. I kept thinking, there's got to be a way to squirm out of this. I was pretty cowardly about it. But God had his finger on me.

The next time we came to meeting, Brother Miracle was up in front praying for people one at a time. I thought, Lord, you've got to help me. I'm standing up there in front with everybody else. Brother Miracle comes toward me. He's putting olive oil on his finger, getting ready to put the sign of the cross on my forehead. That's the last thing I remember.

It's called being "slain in the Spirit." I wasn't expecting it. One minute you're standing and the next minute you're flat on your back. Whoa, what happened? So I saw this guy's hand coming toward me and that's the last thing I remember. When I got up off the floor I heard him say, "It's finished." It's a done deal. Now I can go do this crazy thing that I didn't want to do—God put courage in me that I didn't naturally have.

So I went to downtown Grand Junction where the Satanists had their house. I knocked on the front door and said, "I'm here to talk to Charles." These absolutely civilized, smooth-talking guys said, "Well, he's upstairs." I couldn't believe it—I thought they would have crooked noses and there would be cobwebs on the door and all this stuff. Anyway, you go up these stairs to the top of the house, up in the attic. And there is Charles sitting in a chair, holding a carved stick as if it's his scepter. And there's this other guy sitting cross-legged near him—I don't know if he's his bodyguard or compatriot or what.

I told him, "Jesus can lift you out of this Satanic bondage that you're in. One drop of Jesus' blood will burn all your papers up." He backed away a little bit and said, "He won't do that, will he?" I said, "Not if you don't let him." Then he relaxed. I didn't know anything about papers, but God showed me what to say. Then I prayed over his stick, which he didn't like, and left that place. I don't know what became of Charles. Sometimes I pray for him.

Cicada

1971

SEVENTEEN YEARS after Dad's release from the hospital, it all came back. My sister Charise told me how it happened.

She and the family were traveling home, rolling westward toward Denver on the flat interstate, coming back from Grandpa Elvin's funeral in Topeka. Dad was driving the "paddy wagon," his paint van with two seats in front and none in back. The red sun was sinking. Charise and her brother were clowning around—still just kids (I was already married and away at Bible college). Mom rode in front on the passenger side. The Kansas wheat was flying by.

With no warning, Dad's arms flew up. He shrieked, "Oh, my God. Stop them, stop them!"

Mom said, "Quick! Stop the car." She grabbed the steering wheel and pulled the van off the road.

Dad was in the driver's seat, mouth gaped open in horror. "Oh, my arm! I can see their faces." He remembered doctors and orderlies, and began calling out their names. Told how they had filled the basin straight from the tap, steam-belching fire out of the boiler, and forced his arm under it, taunting him, urging him, "Call on your Jesus." They laughed and held up a picture of Jesus while they scalded him. Dad called out in agony, "Dear God, please help me."

My sister cradled him in her lap while Mom steered the van the rest of the way back to Colorado. He cried for three hours as images of the mental hospital unfolded with terrifying vividness. Attendants in white coats.

◆

I'm looking at a slice of agate my wife handed me. A hollow-centered, bejeweled cave with expanding gray and orange bands. This story is like an expanding galaxy; new facts keep appearing.

Dad pastors a church in Durango. Housepaints to pay the bills; falls backwards off a ladder, ruptures his back; traction in the hospital; loaded with morphine, thinks he hears from God; leaves us in Kansas, heads for the coast.

He used to stare at the angry worm-tracks on his arm. Then one day, seventeen years later, it all came back. "Call on him now. Sing, cuckoo, sing. Howl to your Savior!" He remembered some names and wanted to buy a gun. Waste those savages. But after a struggle he said,

"By the grace of God, I forgive them." Then little hairs miraculously began to sprout on his arm.

That same year in 1971, Dad and I started a two-man enterprise which we jokingly called the "Fly-by-Night Paint Company." For a short while, Dorene and I lived in my parents' attic in Thornton, while Dad and I established the painting business. That fall, a month after Dad's memory returned, he pulled the car off the street on our way home from work and reiterated to me his story about the mental hospital. With startling intensity, he announced, "God has shown me I have a martyr's crown waiting for me in heaven." A torrent of prayer language blasted through his mouth and filled the parked car where we sat. It came from deep in his belly. "There's the witness. I'm telling you the truth."

Years later, I called up Mom and asked her to tell me her side of the story. Mom doesn't believe Dad was a victim of psychiatric abuse. She thinks he did it to himself. I had known for awhile she felt this way, but could never bring myself to ask her about it. Finally, I decided it would be dishonest not to hear both sides. After all, Mom knew Dad better than anyone else.

From her view, the State Hospital in Topeka was one of the top mental institutions in the country, with psychiatric residents trained at the progressive Menninger Clinic, located across the street from the hospital. My grandmother was a friend of Mrs. Menninger and attended a weekly Bible study in her home. Here was a ray of hope. Better to land here than Pueblo.

The hospital calls Mom with bad news. According to them, Dad scalded himself while drawing water for a bath. They say he deliberately held his own hand under the spigot—spoke to his hand, saying, "It's you that got me into all this trouble." They've bandaged him, but he is in a bad way. They're asking for permission to give him shock treatments.

I'm going down the road feeling bad. Dad could sure sing the blues with conviction. His most intense moment of agony could not be shared, at least not credibly, with the love of his life. Such loneliness drove him to the Savior's side and opened gushing fountains of music. His fingers rippled over the keyboard as he sang with unstopped voice: *Anyone can sing when the sun is shining bright, but it takes the Lord to give a song in the night.*

The Fly-By-Night Paint Company is off to a roaring start. The most important part of the day is break time as far as Dad's concerned. We paint for awhile, knock off at ten in the morning, drive around looking for a place to eat. Our clients don't know what to make of our easygoing ways, but we do a good job, so whatever. We find a nice family restaurant and slide into a booth. While we're eating, we notice a mural beside our booth—a harvest scene—and an inscription beneath: "Ho everyone that thirsteth, come ye to the waters, and he that hath no money; come ye, buy, and eat; yea, come, buy wine and milk without money and without price." When we get back from our hour-long break, a note awaits us. "Sorry I missed you. The enclosed check should bring us up to date. The extra $20 is for lunch."

Another time, we're browsing through a rack of Bible tracts in a dimly-lit print shop. We're there to get business cards made: *Badgett & Badgett Painting*. Dad picks up a tract which poses the question: are you a milk Christian or a meat Christian? As we drive to the next job, Dad mulls this over. Don't we need both? Why not milk and meat? Then he gives me a quizzical look. "You know," says Dad, "I had a milk job recently." (He paid off his dairy bill by painting the dairy farmer's house.) "Maybe we'll get a meat job next."

Where shall we go today? We've been repainting signs around the Denver area. We head north and end up in front of a meat-packing plant in Loveland, Colorado. The method has been for one of us to go in to hustle work while the other stays in the car and prays. It's my turn to go in. "Sir, your sign needs a fresh coat of paint. After all, that's people's first impression."

He brushes me aside. "If I want my sign painted, I'll hire some drunk off the street."

I tell Dad what happened. "You go back in there and tell him we'll trade him straight across for a carload of meat." It's a deal. We paint the bowlegged "Old-Timer" with his black, bushy beard, and red-and-white checkered shirt and drive home loaded with meat. We proudly

pull up to the house, where Dorene and Mom have been patiently waiting, our car stacked high with neatly wrapped packages of pork chops, spare ribs, bacon, and sausage.

Dad had been training me since I was ten to be a painter. ("You'll always have a trade to fall back on.") He himself had started at age nineteen in California while attending Bible college. As the story goes, he walked by a paint project, Bible in hand, and stopped to inquire for work. The boss told him, "Put that Bible down and grab a brush."

We masked with newspapers instead of masking paper. Sometimes I got distracted reading the paper. Dad would say, "Did you notice the want ads? Lots of painters are out of work." We cleaned ourselves up liberally—practically bathed ourselves—with lacquer thinner and soaked our painter "whites" in lye overnight in the bathtub. Dad insisted on spiffy white pants and a white dress shirt as the official work uniform. The shirts came from the Salvation Army.

Daddy was determined to plow through this world with good humor while making a buck or two along the way. He kept on painting right up to the day he died at age 67. Kept climbing up and down those 30-foot ladders, slapping on the paint. "Painting hup de house," as he derisively said. There was still paint under his fingernails when they lowered him into the ground.

Death by Drowning

1976

A FAINT STINK emanates from the mud—bodies that will never be found. Cars crumpled into wads like tinfoil. O Big Thompson, you rolling river. I remember Dad's odd way of asking the time: What tarm is it? And when someone asked him, he'd say, "Time all fools were dead. Don't you feel sick?"

These are photos I took at the Big Thompson Flood. A carpenter on a roof with a crowbar. A car perched on a jagged remnant of asphalt road. Its two wheels hang over the edge where the road was shorn off, twenty feet above the riverbed.

Look at this oversized clock, fastened above the door of a restaurant, stopped at 6:20. And the legend curving around the clock in block letters: IT'S LATER THAN YOU THINK. Half the restaurant's gone. Diners were relaxing on the large screened porch when water came and took them away. Man knows not his time.

For in the days before the flood, people were eating and drinking, marrying and giving in marriage, up to the day Noah entered the ark; and they knew nothing about what would happen until the flood came and took them all away.

MATTHEW 24: 38, 39

I volunteered to help the Mennonite Disaster Service for a couple of days, cleaning up after Colorado's worst natural disaster. Whole sections of the canyon were scoured to bare rock—no trace of land, houses, anything. Within a space of two hours, 145 people died.

Dorene and our children were with me that day in the forested country above Big Thompson Canyon. We'd come over from Carbondale to spend some time with Mom's church, which was camped up there. Mom's the pastor, and she loves to camp. It was drizzling Saturday afternoon when we said farewell to everyone and headed home. We had no premonition of disaster. It was a quiet afternoon, a typical day. Mom spent the evening in her tent, patiently sitting out the rain, unaware of the flood crashing headlong through the canyon below her.

◆

I'm reading poetry at the New Bohemian Coffeehouse in Carbondale with a couple of other poets. Chuck Pyle the cowboy singer is onstage most of the evening. His country voice chills me when he sings a ballad about Officer Purdy in the Big Thompson Flood.

Sergeant Hugh Purdy could have raced to safety, but on his way down the canyon, he kept stopping to warn people to get out of their cars and climb for high ground. Down toward Drake, where the big clock hung over the door, he saw a thirty-foot wall of water bearing down on him. He had run out of time. His last words on the police radio were, "Here comes the water."

I helped the Mennonites pry boards from a house half-buried in mud. At the end of the day people from Loveland brought supper for the workers. In the evening we were entertained by a musician who played "El Condor Pasa" on the pan flutes, which, he explained, was the song played when victims ascended the steps for ritual sacrifice.

Motorists flee the oncoming flood. Houses slide down. Boulders, trees. Hillsides melt. Cars bob up and down, rolling, whirling, tumbling in hell-roaring water.

On grassy benches and rock ledges on the sides of Big Thompson Canyon, survivors sit huddled in the soaking rain, listening to the screams of the unfortunates rushing past in the darkness.

The Intersection

1979

IF YOU DRIVE behind the hogback west of Carbondale, you'll wind up on Thompson Creek, where Snowmass Coal operated mines in the seventies. There's not much to see now, just a couple of settling ponds, but back then the place was a beehive. Trucks rumbled in and out. The wash plant was humming. Shifts of miners worked around the clock.

There were two mines operating, Number One and Number Three. This is about Number One, in a place we called the "Intersection." Locomotives carried carloads of coal out to this dark underground crossroad from working faces deep in the mine. A track slope descended from the top of the mine to join coal-hauling tracks at the bottom.

Graffiti scrawled in red over the portal warned all comers they were entering the "Shortcut to Hell." Inside, rusty steel arches shored up an unstable tunnel. The mine had been around since the fifties.

As you walked through the portal, light filtered in from outside. You strode along a plank walkway left to the hoist room. Light bulbs glowed overhead. Strange world, the hoist room. Not just anyone was allowed in there. Bill Lopez was in charge, the hoistman. He was a burly guy with a mustache and a lower lip full of chew. He kept a tidy ship. No spitting on the floor. Bill had a coffee can for himself. He kept everything dusted down and dusted off. He didn't want you coming in and messing things up.

Let's go down into the mine. The cable runs out from the hoist room between the tracks, over the planks, over the knuckle and down the track slope. You crawl into the mantrip just outside the hoist room, scrunch up in these little low-roofed metal cars; they're painted yellow, chipped and scratched. You crowd into one, jam up against your buddies, slouch down because it's low. Lopez pays out the rope and the cable slides over the knuckle. The cars click-clack and rumble as you descend. You're in a different world. No more sunlight. The track slope is very steep. Your buddies' caplights flash around and light up the ribs, washing over chalky gray support timbers passing by at a regular clip. The trip slows down as you slide under the belly of a corrugated tunnel called an overcast. Next thing you know, you're at the bottom.

Here's the Intersection, where two tracks meet. You step out into moon dust, wearing steel-toed brown rubber boots. You've got your diggers on. They're crusty because they don't get washed often. Guys are wearing dark blue denim ones, gray striped ones and handsome brown canvas ones, frayed but durable. With clean diggers on, fresh from the laundry, you look so respectable and dignified. But most of the time you just look like a hobo.

Some diggers are lovingly patched; others tattered. The men tuck their pant cuffs into their boots and tape them shut to keep the dust out. There's the round imprint of a Skoal can in an overall bib. Some men sport white hard hats, some wear green hats, but most wear yellow hats. The white ones are bosses; the greens are new hires. You get a yellow one after you've been there a year. The hats are scratched up with reflective stickers all over them.

The production crew heads for the face. Bullgangers set their lunch boxes on the rib, ready to go to work. You've got track men, guys building stoppings, roof bolters, belt men, pump men, mechanics. The fireboss has already gone in ahead of everybody and signed his initials all over the place with a fat piece of chalk, certifying that everything is safe. He has to record his observations outside in an official record book. The law can hold him liable if safety hazards go unreported. There are many ways to get yourself killed in a coal mine, but this mine is pretty safe.

So here we are at the bottom, a large open area with tall wooden cribs—crisscrossed stacks of eight by eights—supporting the ceiling. Some lean a little. Tall ribs of coal hang over the tracks, threatening to collapse. They're supposed to be coated with white rock dust, but here and there they glisten black where they've been sloughing.

Down here at the bottom of the track I saw my first pair of rail tongs and gave them the name "booger pullers." The sobriquet caught on with the other miners, so I was proud to have added my two bits to the lingo. They operate like giant, man-high calipers. You pinch a rail with these iron tongs and, other miners helping, you huff and puff it along inch by inch. When I first came here, I still had a green hat. That meant guys like Jack Orlanger could push on me as much as they wanted, and there was nothing I could do about it. He had a loud mouth. We'd be packing solid concrete blocks up those steep, dusty, low-roofed slopes, scrunched over, dripping with sweat, then he'd yell obscenities at us. Kick it in gear, you fornicating anuses. Once we were straining to move a lumbersome steel rail, grunting along, and he barked at me like that. A terrible anger flashed in me: instantly I wanted to grab a crib and smash his head with it.

It was hard for me to face my own rage. That night after work, I went to a fellow miner's house to confess my sin and ask for prayer. Since Ray was a Christian, I figured he could straighten me out. "Ray," I said, "there's a guy in the mine that made me so mad I wanted to kill him."

"Let me guess," said Ray. "Is it Jack?" I nodded my head. "Well, don't feel so bad, brother. I've wanted to kill him, too."

The ribs kept sloughing down there, and there was a lot of coal to shovel. I remember standing under an overhanging rib and the coal was piled up pretty deep where it had collapsed. Jack told a bunch of us to start shoveling to clear it away. We weren't too sure we wanted to bend our backs right underneath that rib. Then I decided to just jump in there and start mucking away and not think too much about it. I sensed Jack's approval, and that made me feel good.

Then I was down there shoveling with a tough Spanish guy. We were working under a tall rib, and I had an intuition that the rib was about to give way. I didn't want to seem chicken, so I just kept at it with the guy digging alongside me. All of a sudden the whole thing came

123

whooshing out and we high-tailed it and ran out of there, with the coal right on our heels. "I had an intuition that was going to happen," I told him. "Next time you get an 'intuition' like that, you say something," he said.

The mine superintendent was red-haired Gary Sanders, a transplant from West Virginia where coal seams are only four feet high. He was in "tall coal" out here in Colorado. You could walk around in our mines standing straight up: back east, you crawled or walked hunched over.

Down at the Intersection, the top was making strange clicking noises, like snapping toothpicks. There were signs the whole ceiling might cave in. "Don't worry," Sanders assured us in his high-pitched twang, "it's just bottom heave."

That night the whole thing came down. A section of rock as big as a barn just cut loose and came smashing down. Giant slabs of sandstone and shale were piled in a big jumble on the ground, twenty feet deep. There were boulders in there as big as cars. Someone told Gary, "The bottom heaved last night." It took six months to clean it up.

The day after the cave-in, a lanky Mexican named Ignacio and I were sent up into the caved area to start bolting and hanging chain link fence. Although apprehensive about going up in there, I was also curious to see what it looked like. We climbed between the collapsed slabs and the freshly caved ceiling to the high point where it domed out. The ceiling was wet, gray-brown, and seemed, well, virgin. It had the feel of danger, but wasn't really dangerous.

I remember picking my way down that heap of jumbled slabs when a rock cut loose and started rolling toward me. I ran down the slag pile ahead of it, laughing my head off while it picked up speed and chased me all the way to the bottom.

A dramatic moment came soon after the cave-in. Some major slabs had choked off the bottom entry of the mine. Two gigantic ones leaned against each other, waiting to collapse. It was essential to get in there and blast them apart, but nobody wanted to risk their neck getting underneath those things. The mine superintendent ordered the shift boss, Steve Gatchell, to set up a jack leg in there and start drilling. He refused. You could hardly blame him. The super threatened to fire him, but Gatchell wouldn't budge. None of the other bosses wanted to deal with it.

Next thing you know, the super was on the phone to Terry Gundersen, the owner of the mine. "Nobody'll work under these slabs." An hour later Gundersen himself appeared underground in his white hat and blue diggers to pow-wow with the other bosses. After deliberation, they settled on Ephraim Munoz, an hourly man. Ephraim said sure, he'd do it. The rest of us stared as Ephraim dragged the jackleg and hoses in there and set up to drill. There was an iron-hard courage, a nonchalance, a meekness in the face of death, that won instant awe from all of us who watched.

I'll never forget those killer slabs leaning against each other like a giant tent, lit from inside by Ephraim's caplight, the drill steel plunging into the rock, spinning at a ferocious rate, Ephraim standing jauntily under those slabs, grinning out at us cowards.

Everybody liked Dan Swartzendruber, the bullgang boss. He was the kind of boss who would jump right in there and work up a sweat shoveling coal beside you. He had the complete loyalty of every man on his crew. We did whatever it took to make him look good. One day, Dan and a couple of other bosses got in a flap with the management and decided to walk out. Some of the bosses were disgruntled about not getting company pickup trucks for their personal use. Anyway, these bosses walked, and so all the hourly men walked too. Everybody just wanted a day off.

They decided to go to the doctor and say they were sick; that way it would be an excused absence and nobody could be fired. That didn't work for me. I wasn't going to lie to the doctor. So I showed up at work the next day along with one other guy. We were now official scabs.

It was kind of cool working in the mine that day. We had it all to ourselves. Gary Sanders taught us how to wire charges, and we had a great time blowing up rocks in the Intersection. He taught us how to use the slusher, a gizmo with levers and cables for scooping out loose rock. At lunchtime, he opened his lunch bucket and shared his wife's homemade fudge. When we came out of the mine at quitting time we heard the word. "There's a bunch of angry men blocking the road down there. They've got a bonfire going, and they're passing around the whiskey. A couple of them have guns."

I laugh now as I write this; at the time it wasn't funny. I'm sure I prayed. It came to me to call my pastor, Vick Foglia, who lived in a cabin at the bottom of the coal road. "Could you drive up and wait for me on the other side of the bonfire?" He said he would.

Driving a few miles down from the mine on the section behind Carbondale Ridge, I saw the bonfire right in the middle of the road. Guys were milling like wasps around a nest. And there on the far side stood Vick beside his beat-up green Jeep. He gave me a wave, and I drove gingerly around the bonfire to safety.

Premonition

1979

BESIDES WORKING DAY SHIFT in the coal mine, I taught an evening class for the community college. The course, Caves and Underground Water, culminated in a caving trip to the Flattops, a wilderness area north of Glenwood Springs. We were headed for a wild cave called Premonition, high on the rim of Deep Creek Canyon, which deserves its name, being a full 2,000 feet deep.

We camped in the bottom of the canyon, in the ferns and cottonwoods. It was late spring. Wild violets were blooming; the cold, clear water of Deep Creek gurgled nearby. As we huddled around the fire, talk turned uneasy concerning the day ahead. I assured the students there'd never been a serious accident in my dozen years leading outdoor trips.

Next morning, as we worked our way up the canyon, a student asked, "What are you getting us into?" Since he was a rugged fellow, a Forest Service employee, his question struck me as odd. We were headed into another fine adventure in the Colorado Rockies, and I was relishing every minute of it. I gazed an exhilarating mile across the chasm to the opposite rim, its limestone cliffs still locked in snow. We were far from any trail. Above us, water was already trickling over the south-facing rim. The space beneath us descended into a cacophony of jagged buttresses and amphitheaters, spires, ridges, and steep ravines.

After several hours we clambered to the top, emerging onto a gently rolling evergreen forest at 10,000 feet. Here and there, we trod on spongy ground where snow had only recently melted. Pea-green nubs of skunk cabbage poked through last year's matted grass. We wandered along the rim, searching for Premonition Cave. Then I spied it. From atop a ziggurat-shaped outcrop of limestone, I could see a giant parapet leaning out over the canyon, guarding a hole as big as a subway tunnel. That had to be Premonition.

An hour later we had rigged a nylon sling around a scrubby fir tree and thrown a climbing rope over the edge, hoping it would reach the mouth of the cave. Down from the tree lay 20 feet of sloping karst, interspersed with bits of grass and rock spirea. A sudden sharp edge. Then, nothing. The cliff fell away into empty space.

This massive limestone cliff curved around to the right, forming a rust-pink curtain. I trotted a hundred yards along the edge to a place where I could look down to check the rappel rope. The blue line fell straight onto the sloping ledge in front of the cave. It was already late afternoon. We were set to go down.

Colleen Derry volunteered to go first. She was a pretty, milk-complexioned young woman with long, dark hair that flowed gracefully down her back. She tucked it inside her jacket, then confidently stepped into the climbing harness. I pulled up a bight of rappel rope and fed it through a large figure-eight descender and clipped that onto her harness with two carabiners. The aluminum figure eight would bear the friction of her descent. I snugged an additional rope around her waist as a safety precaution, and tied it with a bowline. She would have a belay all the way down.

Colleen leaned against the rope and walked backward to the edge of the cliff. A few awkward moves over the sharp corner, and she was committed to the descent. She glanced up and smiled, then disappeared into the chasm. I trotted back around the amphitheater to view her progress. She glided smoothly down like a spider for 80 feet, then stopped and immediately began calling for help. I didn't know it then, but the bowline had slipped up around her diaphragm and was cutting off her air. The belay rope—the extra safety line—was too short. Her calls became frantic. A shudder of energy kicked through me as I hurried back to the rappel site. This was it. No time to rig a harness.

Mack Hoover, my close friend and caving partner, had a teenage daughter, Laurel, who had accompanied us on this excursion. Preparing to descend the rope, I turned to Laurel and said, "Start praying." I grabbed a Gibbs ascender and clipped it onto the rope, but in my hurry, put it on upside down. Laurel pointed to the ascender. I righted it, then started down hand over hand. Colleen's voice went deep like a man's. Her last call for help made my scalp crawl—an unearthly groan floating up from some black, hideous abyss. I could see her suspended in space below me, head back, arms and legs flung out. My toes barely touched the wall as I descended the rope. They brushed against a large rock, which came loose, hurtling slow motion end over end, straight toward her out-flung body, then flew past her and crashed on the ledge below.

I came to a fisherman's knot, which the ascender wouldn't go past. By this time the wall was overhanging, so I hung from the rope with one hand while disconnecting the Gibbs with the other, then reattached the Gibbs below the knot. I didn't know if I could hold on all the way down. I continued descending the rope hand over hand, forearms turning to wood, until my numb hands lost their grip. Whirrrrrr, slide. A jerk and a catch—the Gibbs held. The rope yo-yoed up and down. I shook my arms out and climbed on down.

When I reached her body, I didn't know what to do. There was no way to mouth-to-mouth her while swinging out in space. I slid down the rope to the cave, clambered up some narrow shelves, then began hauling on the rope till Colleen's body hovered over me. "Cut the rope! Cut the rope!" I yelled to the top of the cliff. Would they dare cut it? That would be the only chance of saving her.

After a breathtaking minute, the rope sprang free, and Colleen dropped into my lap. I sat on the cramped rock ledge with her limp body sprawled across me pietà-fashion. I prayed with an intensity I had never experienced before. "Dear God," I pleaded, "please give me the life of this woman."

I pinched her nose and breathed forcefully into her mouth as I had been taught in EMT class. Nothing. I breathed again and again, pushing air as deeply as I could into her lungs. Her eyes were rolled back. Her gray face wore a sardonic half smile. Dead air belched out of her lungs each time I tried to blow it in. The horror of losing a student struck deeply into my conscience. I prayed fervently, only to be mocked by exhalations of stagnant air.

This was not going to work. I decided to haul her down from the ledge to flat ground at the mouth of the cave, where I had a better chance of resuscitating her. Awkwardly I maneuvered her body down some small ledges to the cave entrance, then resumed my efforts. I breathed into her over and over again, thinking this was the end.

Then, like the miracle of springtime, her beautiful brown eyes opened and she smiled as if awakened from a pleasant dream. Darkness, then light. It was a sight too sweet for words. The Forest Service worker, Tom, appeared with his grizzled beard and spectacles. "How did you get down here?" I asked. He looked at me with haunted eyes. "Don't even ask," he replied. "I nearly died."

Colleen had hung under a steady drizzle from melting snow. She was sopping wet, and now the sun was setting. Tom and I carried her into the cave and stripped off her wet clothes. We were not only dealing with a near-asphyxiation, but hypothermia as well. Tom and I stripped and made a pallet of our clothes, then lay beside her, one on each side, as the night settled in. Colleen was incoherent and kept moaning, "I'm cold." In this way we spent a long, miserable night.

Next morning we had dry clothes lowered by rope from the top of the cliff. Colleen had a bulging goose egg on her side, which we thought meant internal hemorrhaging. There was no time to waste. Tom would stay with Colleen, monitor vital signs, and give what aid he could. I climbed from the back entrance to the top of the cliff via an easy route we hadn't seen the day before. A student, Rex McGuire, volunteered to run down the long canyon with me for help. It was a wild downhill scramble three miles before we hit a trail and eventually reached a gravel road.

We hitchhiked to Glenwood Springs, where I called my wife and told her the bad news. She called Flight for Life in Denver. I called the sheriff, who in turn mobilized the mountain rescue team. The whole process went slowly, hours passing before we packed into jeeps with rescue gear and headed back to the cave. This time we took a back route, traveling on private property over big, open country west of the canyon. As we jostled along the primitive four-wheel drive trail, the rescuers joked as if on their way to a picnic. I kept wondering if we would find Colleen alive.

We arrived at the north rim after an hour and a half, and the crew went to work setting up rappel lines and a hoisting system. Teeny Jeung, an ER nurse, would be lowered into the cave to examine Colleen. This was Teeny's first technical mountain rescue. Two rescuers good-naturedly competed for the honor of rigging her up for her first rappel. Down she went, over the easy terrain I had climbed early in the morning.

In the cave, Teeny quickly decided Colleen needed serious medical attention. Other rescuers descended the cliff, bundled Colleen into a Stokes litter, and maneuvered her across a ledge to a point directly below the haul lines. On signal, the crew on top began hoisting, and Colleen, immobilized like a mummy in the wire basket, began her slow ascent, accompanied by three crew members who inched their way up with the litter. Several times rocks cut loose above them, and the rescuers interposed their backs and helmeted heads to shelter Colleen from injury.

A Flight for Life helicopter was dispatched from St. Anthony's in Denver. By the time Colleen's litter reached the top of the cliff, we could hear the helicopter's distant pulsing in the badlands to the east. In the alpine grass a hundred yards up the rubble slope from the cave, we made a 20-foot X with red tape, anchoring the ends with packed snow. The chopper grew larger as it approached, refracting a glint of gold from the setting sun. Then the helicopter became a roaring black beast and descended out of the sky onto our landing pad. The doors opened and Colleen was loaded in, still wrapped in her cocoon. The machine lifted off as darkness settled onto the Flattops. The rescue team packed their jeeps and returned to Glenwood. The rest of us spent the night on the canyon rim and hiked out the next day.

Colleen was released from the hospital after a few days, but it took time for her to recover. She graciously invited the caving class to her home for a party. I gave her one of my paintings, and she gave me one of hers—an arid landscape with rough rocks in the foreground and an olive-green thicket just beyond. It reminds my wife and me of Gethsemane. We have it hanging on our wall at home. Each time I look at that painting, I breathe a sigh of relief. Thank you, God, for sparing Colleen's life.

Hauling Water

1979

I REPORTED for duty at the mine the following night, a chastened man. They sent me to work alone at the bottom of the mine in a hole scooped out for the tailpiece. I stepped through the man-door, and it banged shut behind me. Blackness. I sat hunched over and shoveled coal all shift long, never seeing a soul except Colleen's pale face floating before me, ready to depart for the land of the dead. The next night and the next I worked in that same hole with only her apparition for company.

But the real terror of the coal mine was something worse than my memory of the accident with Colleen—worse than the inky blackness, or the knowledge that the mountain could cut loose and smash me. This worse thing raged in my bowels and scoured my brain like a relentless fire. It was the profanity—the slanders against God that turned the place into a living hell.

The men never stopped cursing night and day. They were possessed with virulent hatred for God which exploded out of their mouths like caustic acid, like black fiery vomit. They accused Jesus of being a fornicator and rapist, a liar and a fool. They broadcast their insults with vehemence, striding through heaven and earth with their tongues, unaware they would someday stand naked before the judgment seat of Christ. I pray for God's mercy in their lives and mine. Filth erupted from their mouths thousands of times a day. The men were obsessed with shit. Everything boiled down to this one element. They worshiped it as if they had hit upon the essence of life. It was their "holy" religion.

I came home from the mine each day to my blessed wife and children, my mind in a muddle. I didn't want to poison them with this stuff. I went round and round, chasing my own thoughts, trying to figure out how to disassociate myself from the insistent, damning voices inside me. If only I could get to the bottom of them. Dorene knew there was something profoundly wrong with me. I began to fast. The torment worsened.

A pump broke down in the bottom of the mine, so they sent me with a bucket to bail water. The railroad tracks were submerged; the locomotives had to keep moving. I kept dipping my bucket in the bilge and walking over to a low place fifty feet away to dump it. I did this for hours. Ridiculous. I had been chewing on their blasphemies for days, weeks, months, keeping notes in a journal, trying to stay sane. I was hauling water for these guys, trying to bail the slime out of my mind as fast as they poured it in.

Tenuous

*Save me, O God, for the waters have come up to my
neck. I sink in the miry depths, where there is no
foothold. I have come into the deep waters; the floods
engulf me.*

Psalm 69: 1,2

Progress in cleaning up the cave-in was slow. The roof of the
Intersection had collapsed back in February, dumping ten thousand
tons of rock onto the floor. By the time the men went on strike two
months later, not much had been removed. The accident with Colleen
had occurred in May. By then some of the cave-in had been cleared,
but our method was primitive, and the company decided to bring in
contract miners to finish the job. They set to work drilling and blasting
and scooping it up with front loaders. They had their own operation
and didn't mix much with the rest of us.

I minded the belts. Rocks fell off; I busted them up with a double
jack and threw them back on the belt and hoped they wouldn't roll off
again. Once a large boulder landed on the ground beneath the main
belt drive. I spent hours trying to break it up, but all I got were little
chips. That boulder wasn't going to budge. I banged and banged away at
it, swinging the jack over my head and slamming it with all my might.
I began to take it personally. Lord, guide this hammer to just the right
place. A chunk popped off. Then another. One more well-aimed blow
and it finally cracked clean in two. Hallelujah! I took it as a sign that
God would break apart the slanders that had lodged in my head.

One day while patrolling the belt lines, I heard someone holler in a panic over the mine phone, "Runaway! Runaway! Clear the tracks!" I heard a rumbling sound in the next entry, where the track descended eight hundred feet to the bottom of the mine. One of the mine bosses had forgotten to switch a track and accidentally dropped a twelve-ton locomotive down the track slope, and it was heading straight for the Intersection, where the contract miners worked. The juggernaut plunged downward, knocking over timbers as it lurched from side to side. It tore out a derail switch and finally slammed full fury into the rocks at the bottom. The contract miners, however, had gone outside for lunch and missed the excitement.

Although a few privileged souls like the contractors enjoyed their lunches outside, most of us had no choice but to eat underground. A coal mine lunch room is a simple affair. Timbers are set, two-by-fours nailed across the top and brattice curtain hung all the way around to make a squarish room. Freshly exposed rock hangs over your head. You sit on pulverized coal. Rags, half-empty cans, sputum, food scraps litter the floor. The place reeks like a dump. You sit in garbage and joke and horse around on lunch break. Once, when I sat alone in the lunch room, a scroungy rat sneaked up and tried to steal my burrito. If I'd had my hammer handy I would have smashed him. I hate the way they charge at you with their twitching proboscises and glittering red eyes.

The men like to play tricks. Let's say a guy has set his lunchbox on a stack of timbers: somebody'll nail it to a log so that when he goes to pick it up, it doesn't move. Another one is to open up his lunchbox and put a turd in his sandwich. One time some miners caught a rat, killed it, and put it on a rail so an oncoming train would cut it in two. They slipped both halves into some guy's sandwich. Like the lies I hear around this place, I thought. Two halves of a rat. My duties kept me crisscrossing the mine, checking pumps and batteries. I kept a dusty notebook in my pocket. B Seam pump not working. Cars derailed in the Rings. Holes need mucking. I made frequent stops at the Intersection—that confluence of pipes, hoses, electric cables, conveyor belts, and railroad tracks. There was a lunch room, and a station where locomotives pulled in to get recharged. A lokie battery weighed half a ton and had to be winched out, gravity-checked, and put on charge for eight hours. A dry one came in one time, stinking something fierce. It took a long time to fill those cells, which drank a whole thirty-two gallons of water, then began to perk and fizz.

Sometimes my duties took me to the Rings, a thousand feet further in, to muck a waterhole or fix a pump. This steel-ribbed tunnel had been built when mining crews hit a fault zone and had to blast their way through three hundred feet of unstable rock. The steep-pitching tracks in the Rings made for a precarious train ride. Lokie drivers came screaming through, propelled from behind by loaded cars of coal. Once, a driver snagged his coat on a J-hook while racing through the Rings. He dangled there while the train passed beneath him. So the story goes.

Steel arches supported the fractured roof. These were set eight feet apart and connected to each other with roof bolts (eight-foot rods of steel). The space between the arches was packed with wooden cribs to keep rocks in the fault zone from crashing down into the tunnel. This desolate section of the mine pressed itself deep into my bones.

One night while walking the Rings, I pondered the death of singer/evangelist Keith Green, who had crashed in a plane with two of his children. Grief overwhelmed me and made me sob for his wife's terrible loss. Keith had been so passionate, so uncompromising in his stand for Christ. "I pledge my heart . . . my life . . . my wife for the gospel."

The Rings reminded me of a grim occurrence in the upper reaches of the mine. A lokie driver was standing in the operator's compartment of his locomotive, trying to slow it down as he approached the loading point, when his brakes failed. He just had time to shout a warning before he smashed into the belt conveyor and literally lost his head.

The cursing continued unabated. The vile words stung like darts; their poison saturated my soul. I thought I was ruined. I staggered through the Rings consumed with terror, lost in my confused thoughts, praying to God for mercy and understanding.

On one such black night I walked the steel-arched tunnel alone, deep beneath the mountain, reciting one of the psalms which were my comfort. Suddenly the glory of God enveloped me. He reached down and scooped me up, lifted my head with his almighty hands, and shone the light of his countenance upon me. I could not make my face look down. God flooded my soul with unspeakable delight, filled me with the knowledge of his love for me. I was swimming in oceans of his wonderful love. He kept holding my head up, and I was praising him and laughing.

In my distress I called to the LORD, and he answered me. From the depths of the grave I called for help, and you listened to my cry.

Jonah 2: 2

That wasn't the end of my trials underground—the whale hadn't spit me out yet. But God's intervention at that moment fortified me for the days ahead. I continued to fast, getting skinnier all the time. Dorene says my hair turned copper-colored. I kept traveling through the pestilential darkness, checking pumps and batteries. The Word of God was my daily food.

God showed me a mental cartoon of a mouse barking orders through a megaphone at a brawny gladiator curled up in a cowardly ball. How ludicrous—and such a telling picture of my condition.

A mechanic boss told me to haul a slurry pump back to the rock tunnel. A simple request, but I was operating on the margin. My legs shook from fatigue. The heavy electric cable attached to the pump was covered with mud, hopelessly tangled, and too heavy to lift. I stared at it, weak and perplexed. Finally I tugged until a length of cable came free from the spaghetti pile. Jesus help me! I decided to pull on a bight of cable at the pump end to see how far it got. Slowly but surely the whole mess came undone and lay out just as neat as you please. A miracle. This gave me hope that in a similar way God would untangle the spiritual mess I was in.

The scooped-out hole where I sat shoveling in the dark for three days, thinking of Colleen, had in the ensuing months been enlarged into a cavernous room which was to become the new dumping point for all the coal coming out of the bottom entries. A three-foot-wide conveyor belt would be installed, which called for lots of bolts sunk in basement rock to anchor the huge tail-piece cylinder.

Once again I worked alone in the bottom of the mine, this time dismantling the old belt line. Here and there jackleg steels stuck out of the ground; belt hardware and tailpiece components lay in a clutter. Above my head hung a wall of solid concrete blocks, twenty feet wide by ten feet high, built to prevent incoming air on the main track from mixing with stale air on the belt line.

As I sat on the old belt, taking apart a splice, I heard a tiny clicking noise, like the snap of a twig in the forest. Without thinking, I leaped to my feet and ran to the center of the room, nimbly dodging drill steels and cluttered machinery. When I looked back, the concrete wall had collapsed and lay in a heap in the place where I had been working—a ton and a half of solid blocks. I think an angel guided my feet.

There are so many ways to get killed in a coal mine. That's why the pay is so good. When I was working at Mid-Continent after I quit Thompson Creek, one of the mines blew up and killed fifteen men. Some of those men knew ahead of time that it was going to blow. It was only a matter of time.

To me, though, the really bad thing was the spiritual vileness. Most people wouldn't think of that as a hazard, but I've spent my life recovering from it. For years I've struggled to suppress hateful, unwanted thoughts that trace back to those nightmare days in the coal mine. Some who read this will understand. I think it's an ugly system of abuse that deserves destruction. I pray that God in his perfect time will set the matter right.

I remember rehearsing their curses in my head, trying to make sense of them. Then I'd be slammed with guilt for even harboring the thought of such abominations. It was like wrestling with a tar baby.

INFERNO

Revilings, provocations
Trumpets blasting in my ears
Red-hot hatchets flying

Gobs of spit
Layers and yet more layers of false doctrine
Doctrines of demons centuries thick

Men boasting of their power to defile
Dancing their ritual dance
In a commotion of tinsel and feathers

Stomping the ground
Disks clinking, placating the tio,
The red-eyed rey Moreno of the coal mine

Their curses like ornate totems,
 Hollow logs full of broken bones

The hateful names of their deities
Burning in my brain

I spent a few weeks short of seven years underground. During those seven years I grappled continually with tormenting thoughts of blasphemy. The coal mine became a crucible—an askasis, as our pastor calls it—a place of narrow confinement. It took intense pressure, a smashing flat of my skull in the mud, for God to bring me into a new way of understanding him.

Before those days in the mines, I had been rather smug. On rock climbs, I assumed I wouldn't fall. Years ago on the Bastille, my partner Frank Prescott had called up to me, "Put in a piton now, or I'm going to

untie the rope." We were already a hundred fifty feet up. To please him, I put one in. Shortly after that I peeled and ended up spinning around in space hanging from that one piton, laughing my head off.

In Pentecostal worship services I moved with similar insouciance. Dancing, swaying, playing the guitar, wading waist deep, then over my head—swimming in the sweetness and joy of the Lord. Once I went running toward the front of a church to bask in the divine presence when I was stopped dead in my tracks and forced to my knees by the power of God.

It's fine to scale the heights. So high up there, moving toes and fingers up a bare, smooth wall. The freedom, the exhilaration, basking in the glory of God. But there comes a time when the marred vessel must be reshaped. When the clay gets pounded down so the potter can start over.

In the coal mine I sank to a gaping, speechless place where all I could do was hope for God's mercy. I couldn't dig deep enough to root the problem out. No shovel could dig that far down. I exhausted myself trying.

John Bunyan spoke of a period in his life when he labored under continual guilt and despair. He expected damnation at every moment. "Now was I both a burden and a terror to myself," he said. That's the way I felt. As if there were a bomb inside me. Or broken glass. Or worse—excrement. I saw images of it everywhere. The universe was filled with it. "You're so full of shit," they'd say.

A pump fitting came loose in the upper tunnel, so I hiked up the steep-sloping mine to fix it. The pump sat in a pool of black water. I knelt in the mud at the pool's edge, preparing to loosen some hose clamps with a wrench. Suddenly the presence of God came upon me.

Everything about the mine took on a jewel-like quality—the mud, the dark tunnels, the obscenity, my tormented mind. They were suffused with the fire of a rare, resplendent ruby. Now I cherished the torment. This was my birthright. No one would deprive me of it.

Sublime moments fixed in my memory: looking up to see a perfect maple leaf imprinted in the rock ceiling; walking an isolated corridor to a drained-out sump where uncannily a snowflake—a six-sided plate of jet-black ice—was propped at eye level on the edge of an old board nailed to a timber. I measured the crystal with the knuckle of my little finger—three inches across. It was so fragile, so exquisitely symmetrical there in the lonely darkness.

Another rare moment occurred when I was building a crib in the Intersection, stacking eight-by-eights higher and higher to catch the roof where it had caved. Crouching up there in that rickety wooden tower, another bullganger and I took turns slamming sixteen-penny nails, seeing who could drive them home with the fewest whacks of the hammer. "I'll bet you a bottle of Riunite on the next one," he offered sportingly. "You're on," said I, and promptly drove the thing up to its head in two whacks. I've never been that sure with a hammer before or since. My buddy welched; I never saw the bottle of Riunite.

Another strange scene, this one in the bathhouse. We were working in the mine when the power went down and everyone was ordered to evacuate. You can't stay underground in that situation, because once the fan shuts down, explosive gases start accumulating. We marched out of the mine, happy for some time off.

We had lowered our wire baskets and stripped off our clothes before the superintendent appeared in the bathhouse doorway and announced that we would have to go back to work because power had been restored to the mine. Nobody moved. There we stood, stark naked, nobody daring to move one way or the other—either toward the shower, which would get him fired—or to put his clothes back on, which would mean kowtowing to the company. Finally a brave soul stood on a bathhouse bench and announced that this was the decisive moment—that we should stand our ground or forever be trampled underfoot by Management. It was the only union speech I ever heard delivered in the nude.

"Fellas," said the superintendent, a Britisher named Hayden Winston, "it's your choice. But if you don't go back to work, I'll probably lose my job." Sheepishly, we climbed into our clothes and went back to the mine. Which tells you something about the firmness of our union convictions.

Well, that's enough about Snowmass Coal. The place is all under water now.

Dust and Trash

1983

I'M WORKING at Mid-Continent now, ten miles up the road from Snowmass Coal. I've been here since 1981, the year of the explosion. My job is to haul rock dust into the mine on graveyard shift.

Cold, white dust collects on mine timbers like rime frost, lies a foot deep on the floor. You glide through it, surf through it—the dust is soft like talcum powder. You kick it up with your feet as you walk. Plop, plop.

Federal law requires everything in the coal mine to be covered with pulverized limestone—it's supposed to dampen an explosion. There are rock dust "stations" underground—yellow holding tanks buried under years of accumulated dust. You have to dig through layers of it just to find the hatch door.

Rock dusters (men on graveyard who spray the mine with dust) wrap up in burlap to stay warm while they're minding the tanks. You get chilled down if you're not wrapped up. You push a lever to pump white dust through the lines, then settle back for a 20-minute snooze.

Dust and Trash

Four-inch aluminum pipes transport rock dust to all parts of the mine. They run along the roof at skewed angles, suspended from J-hooks and baling wire. Every so often, flexible hoses hang down from shut-off valves. Here and there, little plumes of dust emanate from quaint pots and drums resembling old-fashioned stills. These are called "trickle dusters."

You wake from your nap and walk the dust lines, opening valves along the way, blasting the passageway with thick, choking clouds of white. You get dizzy, can't tell right or left, up or down. A man approaching from a few feet away—his caplight beaming right into your eyes—seems to be drifting in from another planet. The stuff frosts the insides of your nose, cakes your eyebrows and eyelashes, grits your teeth. It sifts into your boots and fills up your gloves. Sometimes you wonder how, after so many years of this, there is any room left in the tunnels at all—you'd think they'd be totally plugged up with dust. You go out the hole at 6:45 in the morning, leaving the mine pristine white. When you come in at 11:00 that night, the tunnels are coated with a fine layer of sooty black, and it's time to start over again.

Rock dust comes in 90-pound sacks. It's ground-up limestone, calcium carbonate quarried from the walls of Glenwood Canyon. Tons of the stuff come into the mine every night on little rail cars called the "trip." You off-load the sacks by hand, stacking them like sandbags around a combat trench. You work up a sweat. The dust-covered paper slips through your hands and sends a gritty chill down your backbone.

I remember bringing in a load of dust one evening and stacking it at the bottom. A fellow named Mark Edwards helped me. We made swift work of it, then chatted awhile. Mark stood opposite me on the other side of the stack, smiling. The next day a section of roof collapsed and killed him.

‡

I have an indelible image of another man, Big Bird, whose real name was Mike. When I think of rock dust, I think of him. There had been a terrible gas explosion at the mine. Fifteen men died. There were union meetings and safety demands, and the men voted to go on strike.

The last shift before going on strike felt unreal. Gloom hung heavily in the tunnels. I could imagine the white flash, the concussion, the melting heat; bodies strewn across the floor. At the end of the shift we rode silently out to the track, crammed into the back of a diesel-powered Scout. We didn't know when we'd return.

At the tracks we climbed onto mine cars, which were nothing more than sheets of flat steel mounted on wheels. A low guard-rail of heavy pipe surrounded each car. Bags of dust were stacked on the cars four-deep. As the trip lurched forward, and we began our ascent, one of the men grabbed a bag, ripped it open, scooped up several handfuls of dust, and flung them all directions.

Dust and Trash

The tension broke as one man after another grabbed a fistful of dust and pitched it at the nearest smiling face. We were eating it, wiping it out of our eyes, laughing our heads off, and Big Bird planted both feet firmly on the floor of the railcar, tore a sack in two, and heaved a good 40 pounds of dust at one of the slaphappy miners, plastering him against a guardrail. It was no-holds-barred the rest of the way up the tunnel. Big Bird took some hefty shots but never went down. He just stood there unbudged, coated with white from head to foot. I can still see the wet curl of his lip, the smirk of triumph in his eyes.

I'm tired of working. Wish I could be home asleep in my nice, soft bed. The boss tells me, "Clean up that rubbish pile before lunch." That means loading these cars up with trash. Forget it—just let me take the train outside where I can relax my bones and eat a sandwich.

Look at this disheartening heap of steel plates, six-foot bolts in a tangle, heavy electric cable, rotting burlap, dirt-crusted logs, and dusty two-by-fours. It's growing into a vexatious mountain. Lord, please help me.

I stare at the rubble heap. Then a wave of faith washes over me. Perhaps the Lord will teach me something through this. Guess I'll start moving the pieces one at a time.

It dawns on me as I'm working: the junk in my heart didn't appear overnight—it has piled up over the years. Now I have to remove it the same way as this stubborn heap in front of me. Can't let it get me down. Just work on it a hunk at a time.

Slowly the ugly pile melts, piece by dust-choking piece. The logs seem like obscenities lodged in my mind. Scraps of metal claw at my memory; their sharp corners puncture my conscience. All this heavy garbage seems to be covering something underneath. What's at the bottom?

At last, under it all I find a rotten hunk of burlap—a single, limp rag full of holes, coated with dust. What a relief. What did I expect? A bar of plutonium? A magic mirror? A black hole? Something damning? No, just a dirty rag.

Thank you, Lord, for helping me. The place looks cleaner.

Talk Radio

1986

AN ARTICLE in the paper caught my attention. Abbie Hoffman, the celebrated anarchist, was about to reincarnate as a radio talk show host, in which capacity he would "push the limits of free speech." Not that daring, I thought. No one's going to touch this guy. Then it hit me. If he can do it, why can't I? Push the limits, will he? We'll see who gets kicked off the radio first.

I submitted a proposal to our local public radio station, KDNK. My program would introduce a conservative viewpoint into the station's block scheduling, which allocated an hour each weekday to news, opinion and commentary. The content would range across a spectrum of interests: art, literature, history, religion, philosophy, education, psychology, politics, economics, and human rights, and would be sprinkled liberally with music, especially jazz. The purpose of this endeavor was to stimulate lively discussion in the community, and to offer perspectives often excluded from the media. The public would be treated to a glimpse into the world of conservative thought. After all, I gamely suggested, this is what democracy is all about.

KDNK already had a saucy program of leftist commentary dished out by Jon Klusmire. His irreverent romps through the underbrush of current affairs were already well-known and adulated. I thought his views invited confutation and hoped to provide Jon with a worthy adversary.

The board considered my proposal and the answer was – yes! A pleasant surprise indeed. Three years earlier my daughter and I had requested a slot for contemporary Christian music and had been refused. We did get the music show approved after passing around a petition. This time no petition was necessary. An auspicious start.

I decided to kick it off with a two-hour special, and put blurbs in the local paper to create some anticipation for the show. "The most unheard of show you've ever heard of. Live! Uncensored. May 30 on KDNK Radio." "Things they never taught you in school." With the vivacity of an eccentric chef I concocted entrees for the first program. Spoofs, news clips, dialogue, and lots of good tunes.

There would be wonderful guests. Susan Puzio, formerly known to the valley as Rage. She had arrived in the valley with sackloads of peyote to establish her own church in Marble. Then she became a Christian, forsook her peyote-eating ways, and became an evangelist. Chuck Waugh, a furniture maker by trade, iconoclast and wit, who had introduced me to the writings of Peter Kreeft. Paul Bergamini, a local chiropractor who had distinguished himself locally by campaigning against pornography. Paul, too, had a ready wit and a gusty relish for the ironic. Chuck Waugh's wife, Annie, joined us, as well as Sue Blue, John Sercel and Olav Haarklou. Fine companions! Co-conspirators, partners in crime.

I was nervous. What if my brain went blank or, dread, the equipment refused to pick up and transmit? What if an irate listener phoned in and smote me with her tongue? What then?

The fateful evening came and we took our turn at the mike. We sniggered our way through a list of the Pop Hits of the Century:

We Know All About Sexual Intercourse and Everything
The Rock 'n' Roll Thoroughbreds

If You Don't Go to Bed With Me Tonight My Feelings Will Be Hurt
Johnny Crybaby

Whole Lotta Screamin' Goin' On
The Adenoids.

Have I Got Drums For You
Amplified Laundromat.

Let's Have Sexual Intercourse Before Breakfast
The Early Birds

And topping the charts, the mind-blowingest hit of all times, The Doors' groundbreaking "Come On Baby and Have Sexual Intercourse With Me Twice in a Single Day." Such derring-do.

We discussed a study by Rothman and Lichter conducted in 1982, in which a sample of influential journalists and broadcasters revealed themselves to be overwhelmingly in favor of abortion and extramarital sex. Ever hear a serious discussion about abortion on television? One in which the humanity of an unborn child is even considered? We are told that abortion is a "controversial issue," a great debate in which the nation is engaged, but where's the debate? Journalistic curiosity dries up when it comes to this issue.

We carried on like this for two hours, batting around subjects important to conservatives at the time, then signed off, elated at this opportunity to vent some of our long-stifled grievances. As for reaction to the program, weeks of deadly silence ensued. No comments from anybody, except some Christians who heard the show and said it was OK. Finally I asked the station manager, Steve Skinner, if there had been any feedback. He said, "Yes, all negative." Was it content-related, or did it derive from the quality of the production? Steve replied, "Content."

I waited awhile for the odor of my inaugural performance to dissipate before asking for a regular slot. Again, the board was forbearing, and granted me a weekly program of commentary. Tuesdays from five to five-thirty, starting in September. At the end of the month I was approached by the new station manager, Janice Rhinehart, who informed me that some of KDNK's board of directors were unhappy with my program. They thought it was too serious and adult for supper time. Janice's concerns were twofold: 1) the time slot was inappropriate, and 2) the program was said by some to be in bad taste (i.e. references to aborted fetuses).

I told her I was willing to move to a different time slot and understood it might be inappropriate to schedule the show at supper time. I also expressed concern that the board might be discriminating against me because of the content of my program and asserted that under the First Amendment I had a right to free expression of ideas, even if they were controversial. After all, Jon Klusmire was given a full hour a week to express his leftist point of view. Public radio was supposed to be a public forum of ideas. To conservatives, Klusmire's comments were in bad taste.

I asserted that the albums on the studio shelves were packed with messages as adult as mine, that in fact they vigorously promoted immorality. Janice replied that the music broadcast by the radio station was morally neutral. She acknowledged my right to free speech, but insisted that this was not a matter of content discrimination. As we spoke, I noticed an album cover on the studio floor featuring the spread legs of a nude woman.

The outcome of our conversation was that I would no longer be allowed to broadcast on Tuesdays at supper time. The board was offering Sunday night instead. I told her I resented being pigeonholed, as though religious points of view were only allowed on Sunday while the pagan mindset prevailed the rest of the week. Janice said I should talk to Dino, the music director, who was particularly offended by my show.

A couple of days later I caught up with Dino, and we went over the same ground Janice and I had covered. Dino wanted 'listenable' talk radio. I reminded him of William O. Douglas' statement in *Terminiello vs Chicago*: "A function of free speech is to invite dispute. It may indeed best serve its high purpose when it induces a condition of unrest, creates dissatisfaction with conditions as they are, or even stirs people to anger." Dino was not impressed. The show was moved to Sunday night.

So the new show premiered October fifth at 9:30 in the evening. I took a lighthearted detour, conscious of a certain heaviness in the air. I played a Doc Watson rag, then read from the *Book of Days*. How about this nineteenth century remedy for rat infestation: you simply write them an eviction letter. I played a nice little Bolling frolic, "Baroque and Blue" and read some entertaining bloopers from college history exams. Nothing too hardcore there, though it was from a suspect source, *The Reader's Digest*. I followed with a big band hit, "Accentuate the Positive." Then a James Whitcomb Riley poem, "When the Frost Is on the Pumpkin," some spacey music from the London Symphonic Orchestra, and "Tears of Rage" by Joan Baez. I signed off with "Sentimental Journey" swinging lazily in the background.

A member of the board phoned in and complimented the show. Artie, the production manager, liked it. Janice, the station manager, said she would like to hear more of a similar nature. As a gesture of goodwill, my first Sunday night show was a success.

The following week's show, now called *Underground Potatoes*, returned to the serious subject matter typical of my earlier programs. This one featured a taped Cal Thomas commentary on the Mosher case. Stanford had expelled one of its doctoral students for daring to expose the inhumane practice of forced abortion in China. Steven Mosher had lived in China in 1979-80, observing rural life there as a social scientist. While there, he witnessed human rights abuses which he wrote about when he returned to Stanford University. Giving in to pressure from the Chinese government, the university denied Mosher his Ph.D. Where is this academic freedom liberals are so excited about?

I talked about the genocidal conflict taking place in Afghanistan in which a million Afghans had died at the hands of the Soviets. Millions more had been driven into exile in neighboring countries. At the time of this program, Soviet troops had occupied Afghanistan seven years. They were using massive indiscriminate firepower to destroy civilians. Helsinki Watch was reporting atrocities against women and children, human rights violations of all kinds. Booby-trapped toys, pregnant women beaten to death, children burned alive.

Good news: Valeri Barinov is now released from labor camp in Siberia and has returned to Leningrad. I reported on an earlier show that Barinov's health was deteriorating because of his continued detainment in a punishment cell. This valiant man suffered because of the uncompromising lyrics of his Christian songs—stark and haunting like Akhmatova's poetry. The week after first mentioning Barinov, I found a note taped inside the studio door, declaring that "All Christians should be put in concentration camps."

THAT WAS "C'MON BABY YOU CAN TRUST US" BY THE *CREEPS*.

I seasoned these reports with ethnic music—a hypnotic Berber melody played on the double reed oboe, a raga performed by the Shankar family, an outer-space piece by Vangelis. You're listening to KDNK, public radio for the Roaring Fork Valley.

The next show was a humdinger because my friend Paul Bergamini occupied the studio with me. He was in an easygoing mood, as usual. Brawny and tanned with a jocular smile, he brightened up the place like a two-hundred-watt light bulb. He startled me, and probably the listeners, with a headline from the *Denver Post*: "Light of God Shining from People's Happy Faces." The article reported that people were "receiving blessings from the King of the Universe." The normal course of business in downtown Denver had come to a halt for two hours while people on the streets gave thanks to God. Was Paul making this up? No, it was an actual newspaper report from January 20, 1905.

He followed that up with a personal testimony. Paul's life was a waste. Then he experienced the power of God. "Christ can provide you with the answer you're searching for. Give God a chance in your life, and you'll be surprised at the wonderful results."

I punctuated the show with some urbane tunes by James Vincent, Christian jazz artist, and Bob Dylan's "Are You Ready?" Paul said hi to his wife, who was home canning applesauce. "Did you know that the phrase 'Separation of Church and State' can be found nowhere in our articles of government? But they can be found in the Soviet Constitution. Did you know that in the early days of our republic Congress authorized money for the printing of Bibles, and that the founding fathers quoted scripture?" Thanks, Paul, for reminding us.

Janice Rhinehart called the next day to let me know that Artie, the production manager, was very unhappy with the show. He regarded Paul as an "extremist," and was convinced that anyone listening would have turned the show off. He said Paul made me look like a liberal.

Paul thought the show was pretty low-key. He got some feedback from his wife and church members. They wondered why there was so much music and not much talk. Graham crackers and milk to that crowd. So, how do we read Paul—as an extremist or a milquetoast? I think the only offensive element in this broadcast was Jesus himself. He said, "Don't be surprised if the world hates you. If they hate me they will hate you also." To the world, the gospel of Jesus Christ is most unsavory. It reeks of death.

Why is hostility toward God culturally acceptable, while believers must be handled with a chain? In Soviet labor camps, dissidents were considered more dangerous than common criminals. Pastors and poets were segregated from the general prison population lest they corrupt the tender consciences of rapists and thieves. I say bravo for dissidents, for people who care deeply about truth though the world treats them as scum. They are the courageous ones.

On a bitter midwinter night, I stood in a snowdrift without a coat, trying to imagine the agonies endured by Christians in Siberian labor camps. Names of brothers and sisters like Pyotr Rumachik and Aida Skripnakova loomed vividly before me as I shivered in the darkness. I decided to pray unstintingly for the destruction of the brutal Soviet system.

TO PYOTR

Brother I wish you oranges
A hot bath, deep sleep, warm gloves
Vitamins and penicillin, a Bible
Reunion with your wife
And children

A polite angel waiting in the wings
 With the announcement
"Your nightmare is over"

I happened by the studio while Jon Klusmire was broadcasting. Glancing at me in the doorway he said, "Come on in, Stan, and share your wisdom with the audience. Here's Mister Safe Sex himself." In my typically clueless fashion I took a seat by the slim-as-a-willow commentator, who opened the impromptu set with a comment about conservatives bulldozing their way into people's bedrooms, after which he characterized the religious right as a menace to Mom and Joe Apple Pie. He peered at me and asked, "Do you really want to impose your narrow beliefs on all the good folks listening to us this afternoon?"

In a fog I replied, "What would be the nature of the imposition?

"How about the First Amendment—our right not to have your prejudices jammed down our throats?" And so it went. At some point in the conversation a woman called in and asked Jon, "How long do we have to listen to this guy? Get him off the air."

KDNK – Underground Potatoes   Oct 26

It's a cool, clear, starry night in Carbondale. DISCLAIMER. This is mild-mannered Stanley B here on KDNK with another batch of underground potatoes. Tonight we'll talk about those protectors of our hearts and minds, the news media. "AGORA"–PHIL KEAGGY

Reading the Helsinki Watch Committee's report on Soviet atrocities in Afghanistan, I thought: if those atrocities had occurred in South Africa, where would we have read about them in the newspapers? They would have been plastered all over the front page.

Did you know that Stalin deliberately starved 7 million Ukrainians in the 1930s? I recently read an eyewitness account by Miron Dolot in his book, *Execution by Hunger*. This man's childhood experience in the Ukraine gives rise to the blackest of black humor. A documentary film on this subject has won some awards. I wonder why the major networks refused to show it.

This summer I was privileged to hear Carlton Sherwood, a Pulitzer Prize-winning journalist, speak in Denver. Sherwood has a well-established reputation for the investigative reporting of organized crime. Well, he decided to report on the subject of infanticide—the killing of infants. When Sherwood first decided to pursue the subject, his boss told him to forget it. After insisting on investigating the issue, he was given firm guidelines: under no circumstances was he to use the word "infanticide," or the word "kill," or the phrase "starve to death." He was forbidden to conduct any interviews with doctors who held a pro-life position. He eventually found himself in the ludicrous position of interviewing pro-life doctors on the sly, late at night, in the same sleazy hangouts where he used to interview contacts for his crime stories.

Mr. Sherwood doesn't mince words. He describes members of his own journalistic profession as cultural bigots who have no tolerance or even any interest in trying to understand people with a pro-life point of view. You know, I always thought that "bigotry" was a category reserved for conservatives, but maybe there's room in it for the press, too.

"MEAT THE PRESS" – STEVE TAYLOR.

Recently some prominent religious leaders met to issue a statement to the press. Perhaps the most diverse gathering of this type in history, it included rabbis, Catholic and Orthodox bishops; Baptist, Methodist, Assemblies of God, Presbyterian, and Lutheran pastors; representatives of the National Association of Evangelicals, Latter Day Saints, World Council of Churches, National Religious Broadcasters, and others. Together these church officials represented a religious constituency of some 150 million Americans. Reporters from major newspapers were there; TV cameras from the networks were there. If this press statement had been for nuclear freeze or women's liberation, it would have landed on the front pages. But no, these men were protesting the rising tide of violent pornography and child pornography in America.

Not a single major TV network carried the story. They buried it. There are some things they want you to think about. There are some other things the media would rather you didn't get concerned about.

THE TIMES THEY ARE A-CHANGING" – BOB DYLAN.

SIGN OFF Honest, you guys. I like the media.

"WISHED YOU WERE THERE" – PHIL KEAGGY.

KDNK Underground Potatoes Nov 9

TIME. STATION ID. PROGRAM ID. DISCLAIMER. More spuds coming up.

"DON'T LET THE RAPTURE PASS YOU BY" – LARNELLE HARRIS.

Most of you are probably aware of the big meditation event coming up December 31st. I mean really big, with 50 million people participating. This is the one that will usher in the age of peace and light. This will make "We Are the World" look like little potatoes. Our beloved Governor Lamm and Mayor Pena have already signed declarations designating December 31, 1986 as Denver's World Instant of Cooperation.

You have to understand that we're all part of the cosmic brain, with each of us a little brain cell, as it were. According to New Age theorists, if we could all focus our thoughts on the same thing, namely world peace, well, the cosmic brain would get harmonized and we could enter the age of Aquarius—you know, the one with its new Christ and everything.

According to John Price and Barbara Hubbard, two of the moving spirits behind this gigantic meditation event, there are some defective brain cells around that are causing sickness in the cosmic consciousness. Namely those, well, those old-fashioned intransigent types who keep insisting on a right and a wrong, and a personal God who revealed himself through some outdated book. Like I say, we don't want to mention any names, especially one Name . . .

"JESUS, HE IS THE SON OF GOD" – DALLAS HOLM.

"I WANT TO BE A GURU" – WENDELL BURTON.

Did you know that Mahatma Gandhi wanted the Jewish people to offer themselves as a sacrifice to Hitler? (Richard Grenier, *The Gandhi Nobody Knows*). Perhaps while people are meditating on the benefits of *satya graha*, they can also pause to consider the execution of Afghanis taking place while the peace event is in progress. The massacre of 27,000 Afghanis at Poli Charki concentration camp has stirred no great indignation in our peace-loving consciences up until now, so doubtless it will not disturb anyone's concentration on New Year's Eve, either.

As we meditate, we can comfort ourselves with Barbara Hubbard's prediction that those cancerous cells in the cosmic brain will eventually be eliminated. I hesitate to use the word "exterminated." Let's just say that Mother Earth is going to cleanse herself one of these days, much as the Government General was cleansed of Jews, or as the womb is cleansed these days of its . . . contents.

"KILLING THOUSANDS" – ANNIE HERRING.

Several days after the New Age show I ran into Janice, the station manager, who seemed upset. Her friend Susie thought the show should be called "Hot Potatoes." Admittedly, the tone of my shows was sometimes stringent. But there were also moments of pure nonsense, like the time I played three rock n roll tunes simultaneously. The board finally suspended me in December. Then they reinstated the program, allowing me to continue a few months before shutting me down for good in April, 1987. I learned later that one board member, Jon Klusmire, had courageously defended my First Amendment rights, but he was overruled.

Hermit's Hideaway

1986

AFTER working all night in the mine, I'd drive up the Crystal River valley to our rustic chalet in the Elk Mountains. It was situated in a beautiful meadow near Marble, where I had attended Outward Bound as a boy. This was a dream come true. We had built it with our own hands and generous help from neighbors and folks at church. The wood for the beams was recycled from an old general store in Marble, abandoned since the early 1900s. Two-by-twelve floor joists, laminated three together, made stout roof beams for our house. Everything was situated on eight-foot centers, nice and solid.

We had started out in a little art studio built on mine-crib stilts. We had no television; in the evening Dorene and I read books to the children. We hauled water from a nearby spring. We heated the studio with a tiny wood stove and did our cooking and heated our bathwater on a hotplate—spit-bathed with a washrag dipped in a porcelain pan. The 500-square-foot studio housed six of us for several years before we finally built the chalet.

In those early days on the property, we were living out our alpine dream derived from such fantasy-inducing classics as *Heidi* and *Banner in the Sky*, and a glorious coffee table book full of rustic chalets in the Alps. We had also been strongly influenced by Francis Schaeffer, the Christian philosopher who hosted late-night discussions with college students from around the world at his chalet in Huémoz, Switzerland. And we still clung to a vision of self-sufficient living fueled by books on cabin-building and vegetable gardening, and, on the extreme side, books such as *Edible Plants of the Rocky Mountains* and Larry Dean Olsen's *Outdoor Survival Skills*.

Our chalet was nestled in a steep alpine valley with thick woods on either side, occasionally punctuated by long aprons of rock talus. Further up the dirt road from us lay the mostly-deserted town of

Marble, and higher yet, on the flanks of Mount Daly, the old Outward Bound School. I could gaze from the deck of our chalet to the slanted pate of Whitehouse Mountain where I had manned a radio relay station for Outward Bound twenty years before, and where my son, Andy, a few years hence, would spend the summer mining for silver.

Sometimes Dorene and I sang for our supper at the Darien ranch just down the river from Hermit's Hideaway, which was nothing more than a few cottages sprinkled at odd angles in the meadow below Milton Creek. This was the same ranch where we had slid into a snowdrift with baby Aimee in Dad's old paint wagon in 1970. Now we had teenage kids. As saddle-weary tourists settled around the campfire for barbecue and beans, we told them cowboy yarns and sang about the Old Chisholm Trail, she on the autoharp, myself on the guitar.

Hermit's Hideaway. Blessed patch of land nestled among luminous ridges, beyond Mount Sopris in its solitudinous haze, behind the indigo gash of the Narrows. Chang! Where freshets tumbled down from unnamed peaks and bear and elk roamed more frequently than man. We lived there for seven years.

Back in the fall of 1982 we had made our first sojourn to what would become a favorite playland, starting off in our green Toyota Corolla for the tumultuous woods and waterfalls upriver from Hermit's Hideaway. Dust flew behind us. Blocks of sugary white stone lay tumbled among the aspens. Bright yellow leaves fluttered in the sunlight as we wound our way through the jumbled, over-vegetated dogpatch of Marble,

Colorado. Here was the jail with its creaking door and rusting cages, now a play-place for children, and there the general store collapsed in a heap. The unkempt brown building across the street headquartered an eccentric potter, Thano the Greek, with his flowing white beard. And near it, barely visible in a grove of giant cottonwoods, the tin roof of June Blue's A-frame house — June, who as a little girl had been a guest in the castle of Lady Bountiful with her beautiful clothes and pretty bottles and perfumes, and her famous husband, Colonel Osgood, who had opened the coal mines above Redstone.

We drove past Beaver Lake and the mouth of Yule Creek spilling gargoyle-like into the Crystal. When I worked for Outward Bound in 1968, I had walked down that dirt road so many times, heart set on a letter from Dorene. How the letters flew that summer! *Once upon a time a carefree little girl went into the enchanted forest.*

We parked by the mailboxes and piled out. Cornets of aspens blaring all around us. Bright, unspeakable, glittering gold. Single file we passed into a quiet world hidden behind thickets of oak and chokecherry bushes. Feathery grasses caressed our arms as we plowed into our private paradise.

A roar in the distance. Oh, you gladsome river. Muscular roots scrawling across moss-covered ground. Splendiferous carpet. Many-fingered waterfalls braiding and unbraiding. Delectable drop, glass-green pools. Secret bridge, graceful as a spider's web, swaying over a 30-foot gorge. We crossed like porters on an expedition into the Karakorum. Bethany just seven years old—so apple-cheeked and imperturbable, placing one sure foot after the next until safely across. The other three children quickly crossed, and last came Dorene.

Steep scrambles. Oak brush scratching our faces. From the backside of Hat Mountain, acrobatic cliffs tumbled into the boiling Crystal River. Ye shattered, ghastly rocks! Bathtubs of polished schist brimmed with well-tumbled water, continents of foam continually joining and pulling apart. Our minds swam from formality to abstraction and back again while our shod feet laughed to feel stone underfoot. We gamboled in a black tunnel like drunken dwarves, scrambled up rainbow-colored quartzite slabs, coming at last to the "headwaters" of our little paradise. And then we had a picnic.

In 1986 my oldest son, Andy, and I bushwhacked up the south side of the Crystal River, which had no trail, all the way from our house to Marble. What a fine hour of bashing it was, tromping through willows, then pristine aspen glens, hillsides of Douglas fir, and a steeply tilted slope of shale descending into the river, which made an exhilarating challenge. We ran at it full speed, with every step disintegrating beneath us until by a slender margin we reached the other side without getting wet. That was such a jubilant feeling. We bought a can of root beer in Marble and sauntered home on the county road.

Andy, a contemplative boy, liked to sit and look out the window for hours. Perhaps ants would crawl down a pine needle, or a bird would hop on a branch. The trash-talking, rock 'n' roll, football scene in town wasn't so interesting to him; he liked wandering around the beaver ponds and willow thickets in front of our house, where minnows darted about. Sometimes a beaver would slap its tail and glide underwater to some new secret place. He and his brother built a raft each summer, lashing logs with rope or nailing them together with 2 x 4s.

A tall, handsome Swede, Andy closely resembled his great-grandfather Elvin, judging from a boyhood photograph of Elvin taken around 1910. When I saw Andy for the first time he was red-skinned and covered with white "fur." I remember how elated I felt at his birth, and how he squawked when I bundled him up to go home. Now, at 15, he was on the wrestling team in high school, had his own computer, and was testing out theories about aerodynamics and chess strategy.

By the summer of 1986, Aimee had finished high school a year early and hiked over Schofield Pass to Lake City to join the Hinsdale County Search and Rescue team. She worked for a summer camp, guiding groups of campers up 14,000 foot peaks, then moved to Texas to study nursing. She was my tomboy, built like a stick, always wearing blue jeans and hiking boots, never a dress. One of our grandest moments involved traversing a marble slab with Yule Creek swirling beneath our feet. She and I moved like synchronous spiders on tiny holds, mostly in control but sometimes on the verge of falling off. The marble was so white and glassy-smooth, the water so deliciously green.

Alpen skateboarded on the deck of our Swiss chalet, went tubing on the river, fished in the beaver ponds, wrestled with his buddies, and in general found enough mischief to suit an eleven-year-old. Bethany collected berries of various kinds, puffballs, and nettles for nettle soup. She and her friend Miriam had a girls-only clubhouse in an old water treatment tank where boys could visit sometimes. The kids rode up and down the valley on the neighbors' horses. The whole place was one giant playground.

Woman, you put up with me all those years. You and me and a house full of kids, living our backwoods dream. The sweet Crystal lapping by—cold, knee-deep, tourmaline-colored river. Those were some years. The kids could fly bareback. And swirl and swim and build rafts on the placid beaver ponds. Ridges swooped down. The tumultuous forest overspilled everything. We lived there in the middle of it.

Fireboss

1986

THE INERT TOP was hard as flint. He rapped it with his knuckle, but it made no resonant sound—only a cold click. No hint of the strata piled half a mile over his head. It knew not its own weight.

He thought of last night's dream: a large canvas of fauvist pinks and purples with black trees standing like wrought-iron ciphers— the masterpiece he was destined to paint. His wife smiled at him, unabashed and soft as a peach. He fell into such a comfortable state that he tumbled out of bed and laughed. When he looked again, he was alone, twisted up in his blanket. Straining to speak, he could make only gurgling sounds. They'll think I have nothing to say. *They'll think I'm only crying.*

The top skimmed past his head like tight hieroglyphics in a Mark Tobey painting—dry, bone-white, inscrutable. His slow-motion lope carried him along, swashbuckling bag-a-pants man with a fat piece of chalk stuffed in his bib pocket. He used it to scrawl his initials on concrete blocks, timbers, and rusted scraps of steel in the distant reaches of the mine.

He imagined the fireball roaring up the entry, ripping coal out of walls, pulverizing it to combustible powder. Five years ago it happened. Explosion doors flying off their hinges. The ripsaw of multiple explosions devastating the mine. The silent aftermath.

He moved along the passageway into a low room whose sagging roof seemed ready to burst, its old timbers grim under the mountain's weight. Every night he entered this tomblike place—this pregnant room tight in the grip of gravity.

Recently he'd dreamed of the vice principal's office at Mapleton High School, its paneled walls festooned with plaques and certificates and a paddle drilled full of holes hanging from a nail. He stood before the giant desk while sentence was pronounced: "You will be hit hard on the butt with a brick." But he had talked fast, assuring the vice principal he posed no threat to the school. What's more, he promised, thirty years from now he'd make a difference in the world. The vice principal let him go.

In the high school library, shelves loaded with time-worn books faded into the darkness. Right in front was a rack of record albums, including one about tropical plants with rubbery, variegated leaves and coiling tendrils. At the checkout desk he saw a baby crawling on the floor. Its mother, a plump black woman, scooped it up, bared her breast and suckled it. The baby had flaming red hair and oddly flexible feet. Such was his dream.

The mine absorbed all sound. Chips from the brittle ceiling clattered like pottery shards beneath his boots. He would write the book. He pulled the chalk out of his bib and scribbled the date and his initials on an old flap of conveyor belt.

He imagined bodies lying peacefully on the mine floor. Black water burbling deep in One Mine where the gas still seeped that caused the explosion. He had shoveled at that very spot—alone in the bowels of the mountain, intoxicated with the shovel's rhythm, entranced, lost in prayer.

He jotted some poetic lines into a small brown notebook, along with air readings and the status of pumps at various waterholes. A new idea. Poetry. Years had passed since those crazy days reading Kerouac, DiPrima, LeRoi Jones; writing nonsense plays and adolescent verse. He'd spent the last twenty years painting houses, scrubbing toilets, bucking bales, shoveling coal, raising a family. Now words bubbled up into his mind. *Have you ever done time with the boys on graveyard, with the easygoing boys too tired to be ornery?*

He scanned the pregnant top. When will this thing cave in? He pictured Billy's legs extended from under a ponderous slab—caught like a mouse. The paramedic racing to the mine to save him. The crew frantically attempting to jack up the slab, lifting it but a few inches.

While Billy breathed his last, the paramedic burrowed under it as far as he could, but there was nothing he could do.

He walked through the mine looking for portents of disaster, especially pockets of gas. He'd been knocked out by methane before— not a bad way to go. You start laughing, you see stars, the next second you're flat on the ground.

He wondered at that bizarre dream with every detail locked in code. A black woman nursing a wild-haired baby. Who but himself and the book he would write? He would nourish it with the warm milk of his life. He chuckled at the red hair. And those flexible feet. Who knew what direction his project would take?

He saw his father lying in the casket: red with rouge, handsome nose, a smile fixed on his upper lip. He had placed a twig of plum blossoms on his father's chest, leaned over and kissed him on the forehead. He and his brother and sisters stood by the casket, holding each other, swaying side to side, crying. Father, you've gone away. I'm alone in this bone-white tunnel.

He felt like a cut-out shadow. Further down, the tunnel would intersect Three South, that mucky thoroughfare that led to the click-clacking, roaring heart of the mine. But here was complete silence.

He drifted down through the dust and crossed a little bridge—a plank—over a tiny stream. He hunched through the man-door. A sudden whoosh of air. Then he was back in the land of the living. Three South glistened black and wet, strung with air-pipes, electric cables, and waterlines. He measured the air in the gaping passageway, then scribbled the date and time on a flap of belt nailed to a timber. Time for a can of cold spaghetti.

He lay on the floor and closed his eyes. Fields of diamonds. Sweet melting into the ground.

Favorite Things

1993

DORENE and I lived in a double-wide trailer in a rustic corner of Carbondale, Colorado. Pickups bounced along the trailer park's single dirt lane, Mexican pop music blaring. We still had our two youngest children at home. Our oldest daughter, Aimee, lived in East Texas with her firefighter husband and their toddler son. Andy was studying engineering at Colorado School of Mines.

My sweetie and I worked at odd painting jobs—murals and faux-painting projects. We slept on a mattress on the floor, as we had for most of our 25 years of marriage. The family in the next trailer practically occupied our bedroom with us since their front yard came right up to the metal skin of our double-wide. Once, in the dark hours before daybreak, the neighbor and his fishing buddy settled under our bedroom window, sorting rods and tackle and swapping stories. We listened for quite awhile until Dorene finally announced in a loud voice, "Just go do it!"

In the evening I pestered Dorene with questions about her past and wrote down her responses in a memory book. She didn't really appreciate this, being a private person, but she did tell me some stories of growing up on the cold, windy plains of Montana. Her father was a wheat rancher who worked long, dusty hours tilling, sowing, harvesting the hard winter wheat and summer wheat on his spread near the Canadian border. They lived in a custom-built brick home in Cut Bank, nicely appointed with Louis XVI furniture, ceilings of inlaid wood, a baby grand piano, wheat-patterned china, Steuben glass, linens from Brussels, and cupboards full of pretty tea cups.

It gets gripping cold in the wintertime in northern Montana. Once, when we were visiting her family for Christmas, I decided to walk from the house down to the grocery store, less than a mile away. The wind was horizontal and howling, and who knows what the temperature was. It bit hard into my forehead and gave me a headache. By the time I got back to the house, I felt like I'd been on some kind of foolhardy expedition.

Blackfeet Indians live on the outskirts of Cut Bank, their reservation extending from the town's edge all the way to Glacier National Park. When Dorene was small her mother took her to deliver Christmas baskets to needy Indian families. The homes seemed like caves, smoky and dimly lit. As a little girl used to the comforts of home, she was shocked by the squalid living conditions.

Later she worked on the reservation for the Head Start program, teaching children to read. Her parents weren't all that pleased since Head Start was part of LBJ's Great Society, a social experiment which threatened federal intrusion into local affairs, not to mention higher taxes.

Dorene just wanted to help the kids. She was driving a borrowed car—her brother's. She took a carload of boys to the Museum of the Plains Indian in Browning to see the artifacts and dioramas. The boys had never visited their own museum. On the way home they took cigarette butts out of the ashtray in the backseat and smoked them. Another time she ran out of gas on the reservation, and some Jehovah's Witnesses picked her up and started witnessing to her.

Cut Bank was a small town of five thousand people, with a skyline consisting of some grain elevators. There's a section of town that's mainly saloons. Dorene remembers being taken there for haircuts when she was four years old. The barber would lock the door to the adjoining bar when Dorene and her brother and sister came in. He gave the children candy after cutting their hair. Sometimes a drunk Indian mistakenly staggered in. There were magazines and comic books in there that she never saw anywhere else.

Dorene's favorite place was the library, located underneath the fire station. Mrs. Longworth, an ample-bosomed grand dame of a librarian, conducted the weekly story hour. A pack of enthusiastic children always showed up, some of them ragtag poor. Once, at story time, there was a Blackfoot boy eating a raw potato; that was his breakfast. Mrs. Longworth read the classic stories and led the children in boisterous renditions of the Montana State Song, "Don't Fence Me In," and "Take Me Out to the Ball Game." At the end she would bring out a hand puppet, a shy little flannel dog, who peeked over her shoulder to say good-bye to the children.

From the descriptions she has given me, I think the most glorious feature of Dorene's childhood was her mom's cooking. She told me, "My mother makes this wonderful banana cream pie. You'll never find one in the store like hers, that's for sure. It's chock full of bananas, and there's this big dome of meringue on top. It's like a Mount Olympus banana cream pie—I think it's turning into a myth for me now. It would win every pie competition in every state fair, but, of course, she'd never enter a competition.

"She sure knew how to bake. Christmas cookies, hot cross buns, brownies two-inches thick. Every year Mom made double birthday cakes for David and me since we were twins—a cowboy cake and a circus cake. What a job.

"Those moms in the fifties could really put on an event: lots of decorations, lots of food, lots of fun inside and outside. Place cards of all shapes and sizes for every holiday, you name it.Green oatmeal for St. Patrick's Day. Pink cupcakes and cookies for Valentine's Day. Crepe paper in the kitchen, things hanging off the doors.

"Did I tell you about the time Mom put sparklers in the ice cream? There were heaps of ice cream in crystal dishes. She stuck sparklers in and lit them, and fireworks were going off all over the place. The dishes were ruined. They were all pitted. For April Fool's she put a spoon with a hole cut out of it in the sugar bowl. And she put a fake ice cube with a fly in it in my glass.

"Every dinner was a major event. Chuck roast and crab legs and Jell-O and parfaits and tapioca. There had to be a salad at every dinner. Did you have that?" No, not when I was growing up. I thought of Mom working at Target and coming home to the macaroni and cheese I had prepared for the family.

Dorene's father had fought in the Battle of the Bulge. He returned to his wife after the war and settled down to raise a family and run the family wheat ranch. As a little girl, Dorene hoped her father would teach her about wheat ranching, but that didn't happen. Once he took her in the grain truck with him; she counted grain cars while he talked business with some railroad people. Then he didn't take her anymore.

When Dorene tired of such talk, I turned to my schoolwork; I was reading a series of plays for a distance learning course in theater history. Our two young adults still at home had their own social lives in the evening; Bethany was a senior in high school, and Alpen attended community college. Our quiet evenings led naturally to contemplation. I began writing personal recollections in a padded blue book called *Memories: Reflections of My Life*. In response to a prompt in the memory book, I jotted a list of favorite things:

Spending days alone in the mountains, where the only conversation is with marmots— homely, warm-blooded, furry, easygoing, available for a friendly chat. Greeting my alpine friends: sky pilots, silky phacelias, marsh marigolds, gentians, buttery, freckled lady-slippers. Forget-me-nots so blue, they transport me to heaven. A single purple harebell sprouting from a crevice in a high mountain wall. Lush mountain grasses. Utah junipers twisting and turning like bonsai. Electric lichen, rust-red and lime-green splotches floating on seas of dung-gray scabs.

Springtime, which used to get my blood boiling with passion for the rocks, and the crystalline clarity of fall: clear blue skies; keen, crisp air, and radiant, profusely emotional glob-golden glowing citron incandescent yellow leaves.

Wearing dull colors: conservative gray, tweed, herringbone, loden, maroon, drab green, taupe, and khaki. Using strong, deep, rich red as underpainting and always a hint or splash of red somewhere in my paintings. Blue with orange, red with green. Dense blacks and off-whites.

Puppies and kittens and fawns and colts and calves and lambs. Ducklings. Things that light up my face: the truth when it's made evident, the beauty of little children, pretty girls and strapping lads, young couples with sappy grins of pure delight, as Dorene would say, "like melted ice cream." Willowy and handsome dashing couples; mothers with pure, plain faces and very pregnant; tan, lithe old gentlemen with graceful-gait wool trousers, little ladies with their white hair all done up on top.

I like to see Dorene when her hair is long and all done up that way on top with a pin through it like a prim librarian (I once wanted to leap over the library counter and plant a grand kiss on her mouth). In her long, soft flannel nightgown; in her stark and rustic long, brown skirt, green turtleneck. She's so upstanding and regal, and I'm so proud of her. In her short, curly hair and tan face and her curvy, full, round, soft, perfect figure. I love seeing her all kinds of ways—it is always a bright moment when she is there—part of my life. She brings a certain shine.

I like long, loose clothing on people in simple, plain, and natural colors; long, flowing skirts; and beautiful, old-fashioned free and ample dresses. Long scarves and long overcoats. White cotton shirts and blouses full and loose, unironed. The smell of pipe tobacco and leather; the smell of the rocks when they strike together—acrid, bitter, it has the association for me of adventure and being alone high in the mountains. The smell of pinon pitch, of sagebrush, of bat guano. The smell of baking bread, of a kitchen in which spicy concoctions are being prepared. The smell of my wife's skin and the smell of her breath. Talcum powder, roses, fresh sheets just brought in off the line on a sunny day. Turpentine, which transports me back to my father's oil painting days, the heady perfume of creativity. The warm, rich moist smell of fresh-cut coal—productivity.

TENUOUS

Clear, bubbling brooks and splashy cascades and roaring waterfalls;
green pools in scoops in the rocks; smooth, round, wet pebbles; heavily
overgrown banks of long grasses; parry primrose and candytuft; the
sinuous hypnotic flow of the water; gurgling and dipping sounds; clink
and spritz, splash, plop water melody. Worm-track graffiti—ancient,
mysterious, inscrutable meandering, intricate, indecipherable messages
on the dead sides of firs and aspens. The blue and purple and orange
sparkles that dance in the dewy grass and heavily sequined snows set
afire by the sun.

Working-class people. Painters and janitors and coal miners.
Camaraderie with them. Swapping tales. The fellowship of working
people. Their creased faces and deep wells of experience; their
pretensions and unvarnished frankness. The common denominator of
menial, humbling work.

All these things I wrote in the memory book. Our children are
grown now. I remember Dorene there in the rocking chair, holding our
first child while I bathed in the bright-blue rainbows of her eyes.

Bethany graduated from Roaring Fork High in May. She was our
fourth child—our baby. She had attended a small, strict Christian
school in seventh grade and skipped to public high school the following
year. Though shy during childhood, she blossomed in her teen years,
participating in student council, speech team, peer counseling,
international relations club, and swim team, to name only a few. She

190

painted a mural and won best of show at the school's annual art exhibit. During her senior year, she dated Van, a skater friend of Alpen's.

Dorene and I took Bethany shopping at a little boutique under the bridge in Glenwood Springs and bought her a classy black dress with a wide scoop neck and ruffles on the back to wear on graduation day. She painted "Carpe Diem" in smeary, gaudy colors on top of her mortar board. After the ceremony family and friends went to the park to feast on meatball sandwiches. Uncle Mark sang his all-purpose congratulation song.

Soon after Bethany's graduation, Alpen and a buddy traveled to Alaska to work in the salmon canneries. In Anchorage his bag was snatched; camera, wallet, cash, and return plane ticket went up in smoke. They hitchhiked to Kenai, hung up a tarp in the spruce trees, and waited to get hired on. Their campsite bloomed into a tent city as more and more prospective workers showed up. Harley guys, ex-convicts, Indians who fought and drank a lot, East Coast kids plunking their guitars.

It took a while. Alpen got hungry and tried making flower arrangements to sell in town. A church brought a box of meat, so he gave up being a vegetarian. Finally, he got hired by a Japanese company. They started him in the cut room. The Indians had been doing this for years; they had their own knives. Alpen was handling 90-pound frozen fish, working hard to keep up with them. After a few hours his arms were dead tired.

Fortunately, he was transferred to the egg room the next day. Here the salmon roe were raked over big nets, sorted, weighed, and packed in boxes with salt. He did this seven days a week, 12 to 18 hours a day. The Japanese foremen hurried the egg sorters along with a brisk "chop-chop."

At the end of the salmon season, Alpen thumbed it home, riding down the Alcan highway with a guy from Indiana, a girl, and her crying kid. At one point the guy pulled off the road and went into a bar. After a while he came out and woke up Alpen, who was asleep in the car, and said, "Do you know how to fight?" They were surrounded by ruffians. The guy from Indiana jumped in the car and drove off with the roughnecks in hot pursuit for the next 50 miles.

Our children grew up. We grew older. We celebrated our twenty-fifth wedding anniversary by hiking up Notch Mountain, with its glorious view of Mount of the Holy Cross at the top. We had come this far by the grace of God.

The memory book lay on the table. I opened it to a page that asked, "What was your favorite time of life?" and answered readily, "The spring of 1968 when I was twenty-one, falling in love with Dorene."

She had come into my life the previous fall. I was living on a dingy back porch on The Hill in Boulder. Two mattresses were jammed side by side—one for Milo, my high school buddy, and one for me. At the end of the mattresses was a small hot plate to cook on. I owned some books and a leather jacket Dad and I found at the dump. The ceiling was plastered with my paintings from art school. Milo had a poster on the wall, "The Awakening," a scene of voluptuous Hindu maidens in a mind-expanded paradise.

Down in the basement lived Denny, a flipped-out artist, and Wonder Warthog, a drug dealer. I was sitting on a grungy couch down in this dark hole, the floor strewn with paint tubes and sawdust. Denny had been working on a Pop Art canvas of William Penn, which had given him fits—he was going through turmoil painting it.

Into this scene walked the girl of my dreams—an exquisite young lady—who sat on the couch next to me. Rodney, my magician pal from high school, had brought her to meet his bohemian friends. For a short time I was alone with her and asked her, in a mesmerized way, to repeat her name. She said, "Dorene," and I responded within myself, Dorene, my queen. I decided immediately that I should marry her. But she wasn't impressed with me.

Things mysteriously fell together and we found ourselves in love. One memorable springtime morning we hiked up Baseline Road in the dark until fiery dawn crept into the sky; the air blushed salmon pink, then quiet gold, and we knew this was the beginning of a long life together. I had a climbing rope slung over my shoulder and she a daypack with provender—some sandwiches and an apple, a bottle of water. We followed a path through piney meadows to the base of a giant sandstone slab called the "Third Flatiron." There we roped up and ascended to the airy summit, as I imagine lovers have done many times before.

We were married on a sunshiny Saturday morning in August at St. Aidan's Chapel, a small Episcopal church just across the street from the CU campus in Boulder. Father Pat, rector and chaplain at St. Aidan's, joined us in holy matrimony. He was bald and a bit plump, gentle and gracious with a wide smile.

Dorene, as always, was beautiful beyond description. She wore a gray plaid blouse and light-gray skirt. The two white daisies on her blouse represented our love and friendship. I had courted her with daisies, not roses. Our love for each other was such a fresh, wonderful discovery. I wore a brown suit coat and trousers and a brown tie.

It was a formal little chapel with cushioned wooden pews, soft rich carpet, a banister, choir loft, and pulpit. Father Pat was wearing a lustrous white robe. He wrapped a satin band around our clasped hands. As we said our vows to one another, I felt the unction of the Holy Spirit come down over us. It was tangible, like holy, sweet, warm oil poured generously upon us, and I knew to the core of my being that God was putting his stamp of approval on our marriage. This came as a surprise because I had been indulging in sin and knew I did not deserve the blessings of God.

There was a tiny gathering of witnesses at our wedding. It was not a festive affair. The moms had heavy hearts. Dorene was carrying our first little baby in her womb. None of our friends were there, just a few members of the family. Understandably, Dorene's father, Bill, was absent. I had wounded him, a fact I've had to live with and for which I'm sorry.

My relationship with Bill was difficult for a long time. Having a scrawny, barefoot, poet/druggie for a son-in-law—with no mechanical aptitude and no common sense as far as he was concerned—was tough for a war veteran and hardworking farmer to stomach. To aggravate matters, Dorene and I, after flitting around hipdom, became Christians. Not the mainstream sort, but Pentecostals. Sometimes we lived in primitive conditions, which also displeased her parents.

THE TROMPE L'OEIL ARTIST

Deft, deceptive strokes
Hair's breadth of pressure,
        fine-tip brush

Line by line the oak
        footprint disappears

A cardboard palette
        in his hand, he ponders
If my bloody feet had slipped,
        no sons or daughters

Things improved after a dozen years of rough sledding. It helped that I stayed on at the coal mine after the explosion. Bill respected that.

When I finally left the mines in 1986 to start my own paint business, Bill supported my decision. "You'll do fine," he said. I needed his vote of confidence. Within a year of leaving the coal mine, I was painting fancy finishes in a billionaire's home in Aspen. I sent him snapshots of some of my work: faux grain on an antique armoire, faux sandstone, and some fool-the-eye lichen. He drolly assured me that nobody in Montana needed such services.

My favorite sport was bouldering—an absolute passion in my youth. I attacked boulders with vehement intensity, worked them until my fingers were bloody. There was something in me back then that refused to be conquered. I have to work a lot harder now to screw my will up to anything near that degree.

Back in high school we bouldered on the buildings of downtown Denver instead of attending prom. When I went off to college, there was a wacky world of boulder problems on the CU campus, including a frantic 5.10 jam in the music library—a slick, round pillar beside a slick, high-gloss enameled wall. You had your pen in your mouth and, after a wild fight, signed in at the top. Frank and I firsted a terrific boulder problem on Flagstaff Mountain, which we named Indomitable—it was quite an accomplishment as far as we were concerned.

I still get a delicious joy out of clambering around on the rocks, although the Lord had to pull me off them for many years because of my idolatrous passion. I've hiked and backpacked a few thousand miles around the Colorado Rockies, climbed dozens of peaks. Made it up some lovely climbing routes and survived some foolish solo ascents. There was a moment in time when my bare, bloody feet greased a granite face and it looked like it would all be over.

For a few years I devoted a great deal of energy to spelunking, also to the "sport" of survivaling: sleeping in the mud and in caves and lean-tos; eating roots, sprouts, and berries; navigating by the stars; going without food for days; building fire with sticks, and other crazy things.

Now I prefer ambling. Shuffling through golden leaves, listening to the mirth and whisper of streams, picking up white marble pebbles and little, gray, twisted pieces of driftwood, talking to my heavenly Father, glad to be alive.

Dorene and I enjoy hiking and cross-country skiing together. Reading good literature. Savoring the quietness. It is a pleasure to hang out with each of our children, who are now adults—go hiking with them, share a meal with them, have discussions with them about things they're interested in. Join with extended family for reunions and Thanksgiving dinners, play silly games like Balderdash.

I love to study family history, language theory, modern art, Russian poets, prison-camp memoirs. Listen to experimental and classical music. Strum the guitar and sing.

All that good stuff.

Flashback

1997

THE FILTHY LANGUAGE came back with a vengeance. I had gone for seventeen years in relative peace, with vexatious thoughts returning only occasionally to torment me. I had camped all that time on the strength of one simple statement from the Bible: "But thanks be to God who giveth us the victory through our Lord Jesus Christ."

What got me going downhill was a horrifying little book about hell. As I read it, my mind came unglued. How was I going to survive God's judgment with all these monstrosities going off in my head? The more I tried to suppress the defiling language, the more it exerted itself. I rebuked the devil day and night. Quoted scripture verses. Focused on thinking righteous thoughts. But the imp kept at his nasty game, reshaping every thought into blasphemy.

I was so confounded mad at the coal miners for doing this to me. They had ruined my life. I couldn't think a decent thought without it getting buggered up. Always the trickster was curled inside me like a loaded spring. The book had described hell's entrance as a drainpipe slathered with excrement. I recoiled in pain at the sight of anything brown. Mentally I strove to protect all that was pure from the vandal's fingers. Why was this happening?

My conscience spun like a jet engine, its supersonic razor blades shredding my brain to a pulp. I had been out of the mine for years, but if I closed my eyes I'd be right back in the swirling darkness. I kept seeing a man's face, contorted with rage, eyes bulging. I didn't know his name anymore, but I remembered following him down a tunnel when he turned and roared his most powerful blasphemy at me. His face was frozen into a permanent grimace. He had sacrificed his humanity to the demon of the mine.

Clanking coal mine. Sewage spigot. Subterranean city where they spit on the name of the Holy One. I had kept its outrages buried for years. Now they erupted like booby traps. I curled into a ball on the floor of our trailer and retched and groaned and screamed from my gut, "I HATE IT! I HATE IT!"

Psychologists speak of unwanted thoughts. I became an expert on that subject. I was hyper-alert every minute, wondering: what are the implications of my most recent thought? How might it be distorted into some piece of damnable impudence? I must preempt every wicked thought by thinking of it first and formulating a comeback before the devil can accuse me of it. If I don't, it will slam me. I was playing a desperate game of one-upmanship with the devil.

I remembered the place in the mine where it first began to dawn on me that I was in serious spiritual trouble. I had been minding pumps in an upper entry at Snowmass Coal, close to the working face. We were draining water away from an impending flood—millions of gallons of accumulated water in the old Marion Gulch mine, dormant for sixty years—toward which we had steadily mined. The production crew kept test drilling ahead, trying to prevent a breakthrough into the old Marion Gulch works. Wet coal glistened on the floor of the narrow entry. A ditch chiseled into the low rib channeled water out to a series of collecting pools whence it was pumped to the bottom of the mine and finally up to the surface. It all seemed so primitive. And the water flowed so inexorably, so quickly, like mercury. I began to realize that the insidious streams trickling through me would dam up and eventually break.

These guys weren't just blowing off steam. I knew their words had decipherable content that couldn't be ignored. Why did they treat Jesus this way? How could they smear their filth on Jesus Christ, the blessed Savior, my personal friend? How could anyone be that wilfully malicious and ignorant? How could they hate God that much? The intensity of their hatred was dumbfounding. There was no neutral ground for me to stand on—no dispassionate stance that would permit me to ignore their hostility to God's holy name. The coal mine had a most wretched answer to Jesus' question, "Whom do men say that I the Son of Man am?" It deemed the greatest treasure worthless. Jesus taught that by our words we will be acquitted and by our words we will be condemned. How could we survive his judgment? Every day I cried out, God please help me. Please deliver me from condemnation. Please deconstruct this insane system of abusive language.

I was alone at the dining table in our doublewide trailer while Dorene visited family in Montana. The latest round of blasphemy attacks had stung me real good. As I sat there in a seething rage I became very aware of the presence of God. A paralyzing awe crept upon me as I realized the impossibility of moving a muscle without violating his holiness. Every move involved some kind of scandal. A terror gripped me, perhaps like the terror experienced by Isaiah when he said, "Woe is me! I am undone, for I am a man of unclean lips." How could I even live? I sat for some time like that until finally a message came to me, penetratingly clear: "I am the Lord. I change not." That came straight from the word of God. I recognized the Spirit of Jesus chiding me the way he did when he asked his disciples, "Don't you remember what the Scriptures say?"

As the years roll by, I have come to cherish that moment in the trailer. It marked the beginning of a radical change in my understanding of the nature of God. There at that humble wooden table God confronted me with his inviolable holiness. There was nothing I or anyone could do to change it, nor had I any power, apart from God, to change myself. My will-tightening exercises, my efforts to make myself holy, to make "right choices" in my thinking, to shield myself from contamination, had no power to sanctify me in the presence of the unchanging Holy One.

With the hands of a master potter he continues to reshape me according to his own good pleasure. What a comfort to know that his is the superintending hand. I am not the author of my own salvation. By his eternal decree he has called me, beget me, set me apart for himself. The bedrock of my salvation is God himself, not me. Not my decision, sincerity, zeal, consecration, determination, or anything else about me. I have this treasure in an ungainly body, as if in a clay pot, to show that the presence of God in my life is a gift from him, not something I have manufactured. Pots don't shape themselves. Dead men don't resurrect themselves. Everything I have I owe to the grace of God.

My continuing delight is to learn of God every day. I can never get enough of the gospel, of good, sound preaching and teaching from the word of God. I am blessed to have a life-mate who shares this passion with me. Dorene and I both see that man cannot redeem himself, that man is by nature an enemy of God, and only supernatural intervention can change this.

As for the dirty language, God has taught me a thing or two about that. Take for example the wretched word *shit*. There is such contempt encapsulated in this tiny word which ostensibly means nothing more than dung, yet it stings like a scorpion. We taint one another with it, inject each other with its poison. One man essentially says to another,

"I regard you as worthless dirt. You are as vile as the waste that comes out of my body." But dirt, after all, is what we're made of.

Our food comes from the soil. We partake of its bounty. We savor, chew and swallow our food, which gets broken down by digestive juices so the nutrients can be absorbed into the bloodstream. The residue from this process, waste, passes out of our bodies and returns to the ground where it falls apart and becomes soil once again. One of life's many cycles. Where is the scandal?

Yet waste does scandalize us. It stinks and it's toxic. It reminds us of our destiny. Someday our bodies will disintegrate and return to the earth, just as our waste does. We are destined for the dirt, our bodies at least. Ashes to ashes, dust to dust.

We live on planet Earth in bodies made of clay. That's wonderful as far as I'm concerned. We are fleshly beings, gravitationally attached to a six million trillion ton ball, its stone crust topped with layers of various kinds of dirt: humus, sand, fine-textured silt, hardpan the color of terra cotta, sticky clay—byproduct of feldspar and mica, iron silicates broken down to rust-red soil. Basic gritty stuff. The stuff we're made of.

~~

We say of a practical fellow that he's down to earth. He's got his feet flat on the ground. We appreciate a solid argument, one that is grounded in fact. We value solid friendships. Mass, density, solidity—virtues on which we depend. The material world is God's idea, the miraculous result of his fiat command—material coming forth from nothing.

The coal miners had me buffaloed for a long time with their excrement-preoccupation. Then I realized that "shit" amounts to nothing more than dirt, at least at the material level. Now we've got grown-up, intelligent people—not just in the coal mine—walking around invoking dirt as if it were some kind of magic mantra, reminding us that dirt really exists, that food comes from the soil, and right now—horrors—we are actually digesting animal and plant matter in our stomachs and intestines, much of which will be eliminated as waste.

Of course, there's more to it than that. People aren't just thinking of material waste when they say "shit." Next time you hear someone say that word, listen to the bitterness in their voice. Dung; mud; dirt—they just don't pack the same venom. Imagine an action hero curling his lip and snarling, "Dung!" Nobody would be impressed.

I'm coming around to a proposition: that far from being a descriptor with its referent in the soil, this word is a well-honed weapon designed to inflict spiritual damage. It denies the spiritual dignity of man by reducing him to mere material. It's a kind of missile, carrying a payload of boiled-down hate. It whooshes off the launching pad with a shhhhhh, its rocket engines powered by human fury, navigating interpersonal space in a fraction of a second, piercing the heart with an explosive "t." There it lodges, barbed like a punji stick.

Bingo! One man's spite infects another. It makes a grand claim for itself, imbuing the speaker with a sense of godlike power: he imagines he can mow down his enemies like a Daisycutter and reduce the universe to rubble. This is the myth. Our strutting hubris.

I'm fairly convinced that obscene language put my father in the mental hospital—that and his terror of hell. He told me more than once that the asylums are full of people who think they have committed the unpardonable sin. Dad had a particular way of dealing with the insistent lies in his head—he wrote them down. Not so far removed from Socratic self-examination: examine the lies you're being told. Dad delighted in setting the devil's accusations down in plain English where he could laugh at their manifest foolishness.

This practice proved invaluable during my dark days. I filled many a notebook with ravings from the coal mine and disentangled them—decoded them—one by one. Francis Schaeffer's teachings were helpful. What's the claim? What's the antithesis? The truth always lay in the antithesis. Whatever they claimed was always opposite the truth. I wrote my entries in miniscule handwriting and somewhat veiled language to protect, not myself, but innocent readers from pollution. I treated it like radioactive waste.

God marvelously intervened for me in teaching me how to analyze these insulting terms until they lost their power to torment. Day by day, he revealed new aspects of the semantics of abuse, highlighting various twisted claims and contrasting them with Scripture.

Take the debasing term "asshole." Well, that's a crude thing. But think of how foolish it is. A person is a human being, a living entity, not a hole. A hole can't exist without sides. To be a hole is to be nothing at all. To claim that someone is a hole is to deny everything real and true about that person—his value, purpose, personality, dignity, accomplishments, aspirations, history, his origins and destiny, his emotional and psychological makeup, the physiological systems that support his life. And what is an ass? Does having buttocks make a person wicked or worthless? Try living without them. Presumably the abuser himself has an "ass" or he wouldn't be able to stand up or sit down. The Bible says that God has arranged all the parts of the body just as he wanted them to be. The parts we think of as unpresentable are actually treated with special modesty. Every part plays its vital role.

The obscenity I'm describing is part of a barbarian worldview which has no patience with theology. It doesn't know the difference between God and dirt. Sure, there are deities of sorts in the barbarian pantheon, but whatever their masquerade, they are in reality spirits of pride, hatred, and rebellion. Milton described them over three centuries ago: "Perverse . . . monstrous . . . prodigious . . . abominable

. . ." Barbarians want freedom to travel—inside your head. Yield to truncheon's song. Many a workplace, not just the coal mine, doubles as a shrine for pagan deities. Attention! At the sound of the sulfurous oath all shall prostrate themselves.

Big deal, some might say. What's the big deal about such language? But it fails to be important only if truth is unimportant. If truth is unimportant, then we may as well all take a flying leap. Obscene language, profanity, imprecation, false swearing, whatever name one gives it—weaves a spider's web of systematic abuse. It's verbal rape. It's a false religion. It's a form of oppression.

I spent many years begging God for insights into this hateful phenomenon. I prayed many times, "Lord, demythologize this for me. Please undo it. Take the sting out." It was a matter of psychological and spiritual survival. God abundantly answered my prayers, bit by bit, over the years. It was torture, but with a purpose. In my life I had no choice but to deal with it.

A friend who served in Ethiopia as a medical missionary tells of a woman riddled with cysts deposited by worms throughout her intestinal tract. The situation looked hopeless, and my friend thought it best to "close her back up," but a fellow doctor began injecting the cysts with formaldehyde one at a time, until after a lengthy ordeal she returned to the land of the living.

In 1997 I drew a portrait of myself as a shattered man, as good as dead, with a dialogue balloon coming out of my mouth muttering, "Please help me." It looked more like a shriveled plastic bag than a human face. Dorene saw this picture years later and, not recognizing her own hubby as the subject, asked me to get rid of it. At the time the portrait was drawn, I felt like so much rubbish. Like a dead dog.

I believe it's my job to think about vile language and write about it, for one thing because of what it did to my dad. He had sensitive ears, and he loved Jesus. He delighted to sing and play under the unction of the Holy Spirit. He sometimes went into a trance and played wave after rippling wave of ecstatic, heavenly music just on the black keys of the piano. He was always theorizing about light and color and sound—advancing and retreating colors and color "surprise," chord progressions on the guitar—and the way sensations entered the soul through the "eargate" and "eyegate." The way his fellow painters disparaged the holy name of Jesus was a source of deep torment to him.

I've studied language and communication a modest amount. However, the real secret of obscene language has nothing to do with deconstructive theory, but with the Word of God, which deconstructs us all whether we like it or not. Perhaps I sound self-righteous. But I'm just as riddled with sin as the next guy. That's one of the maddening things about vulgarity. To oppose it makes a person seem super-spiritual. But God alone is righteous.

I get frustrated because I have a lot to say and people often don't want to hear it. Here's where writing comes in handy. OK. I'll just be quiet and put down my ideas down on paper. Then, if anybody wants to read it, they can. If not, I haven't imposed on anyone. Writing is a way of staying civil and not going crazy.

I have a voracious appetite for knowing and being known, which can be dangerous. It can get me in trouble. In its bad form (when it's extended too far), it's the sin of concupiscence, which, though hard to pronounce, is elementary to my nature. It's wanting more and more and more of experience. Wanting to know too much. Wanting to have too much. Not knowing when enough is enough. It's related to the tenth commandment: do not covet.

Also, I have a lot of curiosity and so I like to ask people questions—get to know what they believe, what they're firmly convinced of, what their experiences have been. I'm an interviewer. I'm writing an oral history about the coal mines in our valley. These reticent old coal miners reluctantly let me in their houses. We get to talking, and before you know it, the time is up and they still have more stories to tell. This is what makes life worth living.

I love to engage in debate with people. You convince me, I convince you, whatever. Just so we listen to each other and think about what the other is saying. I like to be forced to be more clear in my thinking. I run my classroom like this—it is an argumentative classroom. I want the students to give reasons for what they think. I want them to push back. I'm not God. I don't have all the answers. If they can persuade me, great. But I don't tell them that there are no right answers. Our joy is in pushing each other into knowing more and more of the truth.

This is the guts of writing. Not flowery language. Not even creativity. But getting down in the lowdown dirt, breaking up the ground, learning what the truth is about things. What makes sense, what doesn't. That's where the writing comes from that counts.

Snap. I'm back in the mine. The miner, a gigantic machine on caterpillar tracks, chortles and roars and chews its way through the mountain like a dinosaur chewing up mulch. It's powered by 550 volts coming off the power center through a thick trailing cable manhandled by the miner helper—a human being and not a machine— who drags the cable through the mud and hangs it on J hooks as the big machine chews deeper and deeper into the coal seam. As the miner progresses, new 'top' opens up, which must be supported by timbers and eventually roof bolts. The miner helper works close to the face, not far behind the rapidly spinning head—the business end of the mining machine—which whirrs and rattles, bristling with carbide-tipped teeth. Coal flies, black dust spumes out, the ancient mountain shudders, groans, pops, and booms.

The miner helper hustles to keep up with the voracious machine. He shovels down to the hard, measures up to the roof, runs back to the timber pile and cuts a timber to size, hauls it to the face and sets it in the hole, tops it with a wooden cap and wedge which he slams in tight with the head of an axe. The whole crew is revved to produce. Get her in the black.

Tension is running high. The mechanic is taking too long on a repair. He cuts quite a figure at 6' 3" and 270 pounds, sporting a flamboyant walrus mustache. He's not used to being pushed around. The miner helper, no flyweight himself, fires an inflammatory remark at the mechanic. Next thing you know they're wallowing on the ground, out of control. Rough-housing is forbidden in the mine. If you get into a fistfight, you're both fired. But that's not slowing these two down, and we've got a ringside seat. Timbers fly. Cans get knocked over. They're both flopping around, having a good time. The objective, as in frontier days, is to bite the other guy's ear. Nobody's going to rat on them, not even the section foreman who stands right there watching. A buggy (fast-moving coal-hauling machine) comes whirring around the corner and they have to break it up.

"One thing I can say," drawls the mechanic as he straightens his coveralls, "is you didn't bite my ear."

⌣

Here's a strange story from the workplace. As an apprentice painter in Los Angeles in the 1930s, Dad observed a fellow painter openly weeping and singing praises to Jesus on the job. Dad was so moved that he prayed, "Lord, whatever that man has, I want it." Dad saw the man's tender relationship to Christ, but not the circumstances God had used to bring him into that yielded condition. In answer to Dad's prayer, God wrought changes in his heart over the ensuing weeks and months. But more than that, I believe Dad's prayer explains what happened to him for the next fifty years. It was a softening process that spanned a lifetime.

The reason I went to work in the mines was to tackle something wicked there. Like Samson itching for a fight. Something beckoned to me. I had no idea it would become a lifelong struggle. That I'd end up clinging to the Bible like a life preserver in a sea of excrement, or spend years learning to defuse linguistic time bombs, all to continue a task begun by my father.

A memory of Dad in his later years: he's wearing spectacles partway down his nose, sitting under a reading lamp, scrutinizing Wuest's *Treasures of the Greek New Testament*. He looks like a rabbinic scholar. He's underlining passages about the grace of God, writing notes in the margins.

The last time I saw Dad, he and I rolled off the couch laughing at Buster Keaton, deadpan comedian flickering on the wall. We played supernatural chess, pieces collapsing like dominoes. Now a great heart-shaped wasp's nest hangs on the wall of my memory: fine sheaves of gray, translucent paper pierced by a dozen wire-thin fingers. Dad, you taught me to write lies down, nail them down, make them squirm on paper. But I'm weary of years gathering evidence against the damning voices.

Down at the Blue Acacia

2006

MY WIFE AND I raised our kids here in the Crystal River Valley, high in the Colorado Rockies. We have our special places here, our gorges, deep pools, and secret trails hidden away from the public. We've grown old with our friends, know their joys and hardships.

Dorene and I have our own quaint idea of fun, which sometimes involves going up to Paige and Margie's place, a cabin on the Crystal River, where we sit around the table telling jokes and stories, drinking coffee and scarfing homemade pie. We like to discuss theology—we share a Calvinist perspective—and politics—our brand is conservative. Paige is a slender man, but a stout thinker. He questions things, especially his own assumptions. When the sermon's over, he's the one who stands up in church to ask a challenging question.

When Mollie and Lora, their daughters, are home from college, we play speed Scrabble. Whenever they're around, lots of extra pastries are on the table, as well as homemade candy. We've known them since they were babies. With speed Scrabble, we don't use a board, just mountains of tiles and everybody's going at once.

After gorging ourselves and playing games, we go upstairs and break out the musical instruments. A fire is crackling in the wood stove. Lora and Mollie play their fiddles. Paige plays harmonica. I plug away on the guitar. Usually there are several other folks playing one instrument or another. We're singing about that old-time religion, the kind that makes you love your neighbor, and about the bright mansion waiting for us in heaven. I love that old-time gospel music, the kind Daddy taught me to play. The room pulses with warmth. We pour our hearts into it.

Sometimes Paige and Margie go dancing with us, but lately it's hard to get them to go. Paige figures he gets enough exercise traipsing in the cow pasture.

I like to grab my honey around the waist and swing her around at the community dance, her bright blue eyes sparkling at me. I'm still nimble on my feet after all these years. Dancing, that is. Dorene says I walk too slow, and it does seem I've slowed my walk down to a crawl.

We get slap happy at the dance, down at the Blue Acacia. It's an old brick building, the old Masonic Lodge, with a creaky wooden floor. When that banjo kicks up, I can't stand still. Double bass, mandolin, guitar players—there's a dozen of them up on stage. The caller's in charge, having a good time.

"All you gents go down the outside."

We strut to beat the band, down the hall and back again. Guys all freshly shaven and smelling of cologne; some in cowboy get-up with big belt buckles; a geezer in bib overalls; one guy's unbuttoned shirt hanging down—he's glistening with sweat. We strut like a bunch of peacocks.

Ron, the old coal miner with his brambly beard, stoops a little when he dances just to stay at eye level with his partner. Chad, the fourth grade teacher, dances barefoot, nimble as a faun. The Baker family is usually there—home-schoolers from Rifle. And Doctor Clark, the retired astronomy professor from the community college. He's wonderfully tall—taller than everybody there, and wears a serene expression as he glides around the hall with his wife, Rosemary. It's a sweet comfort to run into these people at the dance, over and over again.

"Join hands and circle to the left; now circle to the right."

We stomp our feet. Let out a yip.

I like to swing the ladies around—their skirts flying out. Chubby ones, young ones, old ones. The old ones are so graceful, and the young ones are so frisky. And there's this sweet blind gal who's always right there with her hand out at the right time, and she's smiling away.

"Honey, let's take a break." Dorene and I walk down the front steps out into the cool night air and drift around town awhile, talking our quiet talk under the dark pines. "I'm only good for one more," I tell her. She agrees. We're not night owls, that's for sure.

Back in the hall it's hot again. "This was Thomas Jefferson's favorite," announces the caller, and he cheerleads us through the Virginia Reel. Oh yeah, I love that. We're just like kids sashaying down the line, skipping, feet flying, our hearts big red cinnamon lollipops. We're mopping sweat, trying hard to keep up. Just when I think I'm about to keel over, the dance comes to an end. It's quiet and dark in the car as Dorene and I drive home. We've had our little bit of hillbilly fun, and we're satisfied. As we pull up to the house, the moon shines on Mount Sopris. The Crystal River laughs behind a long row of black cottonwoods. We are glad God has placed us here in this valley.

Heritage

2010

I CAN STILL see two pairs of eyes gazing down at me from the clouds. Dorene lay on the grass beside me, both of us reclining under an enormous tree looking up at the sky, the tree swooping heavenward, spreading its gigantic arms. She was the first and only girlfriend I ever had. It was springtime; we were carried away with love. An overwhelming force had swooped us up and deposited us on the campus lawn.

This was Boulder in the 1960s, when "love was all around," as they say. But we weren't merely following a popular trend; we were afloat in a real ocean whose waves were catapulting us toward some unknown continent. We had been whisked away by mutual consent to a realm of sensational, oceanic feelings—to a kingdom whose boundaries were swiftly expanding. We had gotten acquainted in the fall; now it was April, and we were too helpless to say what was happening to us, so we lay there looking at the sky.

Sure, we had taken drugs off and on, but this day we were sober, at least as sober as two lovers can be, and all things around us—the red flagstone buildings of the University of Colorado, the magnificent landscaping, students strolling to class—looked as they did every day. Up in the sky, however, amid the leisurely clouds, two pairs of blue eyes were gazing down. I knew by their imperturbable innocence that they were children's eyes. And I knew somehow that this was no droll fancy, but that I was actually looking into the eyes of my future children.

Tumultuous as our love affair had been, it was not destined to end in the manner of so many popular songs. We would be married and have a family. I knew it just as sure as those eyes looking down at me. Yet, unmistakable as this vision was, my sweetheart did not see it. I don't even remember if I mentioned it to her. In due time we were blessed with two blue-eyed children, a girl and a boy. They're in their forties now. Our daughter Aimee is the mother of four boys. Our son Andy is a physicist. After a few years two more children arrived, Alpen and Bethany, with dark, wavy hair and green eyes. The Bible says children are a heritage of the Lord. Ours came in two batches, one announced and one unannounced.

Sometimes when I look at one of our children's faces, I marvel that my wife and I have so miraculously blended into another being, that an independently functioning person, a unique soul, has resulted from our bone-to-bone genetic dialogue. We are exhilarated, sometimes terrified, by our children. We know them well, but they are still a mystery to us. They have dreams of their own, yet these children bear our dreams into the future.

Still Standing

2010

WHEN I STARTED writing this, fire was still racing through the foothills of Boulder. I wondered if a certain house Dad and I painted in the early 70s would survive. Also, I wondered about a little shack in Boulder Canyon where my wife and I had lived with three small children. The tumble-down shanty sat on a hillside dotted with ponderosas, yuccas, and prickly pear. We fetched water from a cistern which dried up later that fall. I remember hunching down there with a hammer and chisel in pursuit of the receding water table. We ended up hauling our water from Boulder Creek.

I have a photo of Dorene proudly smiling in front of Boulder Falls in the spring of that year, very pregnant with Alpen, our third child. He came along supernaturally; she laughed through the whole delivery and has always claimed it was painless.

Dad and I had started a paint company the year before. A luxury home in the Boulder foothills was our first major painting project. The owner, who had fought in World War II, suffered from chronically cracked lips, a result of dehydration he experienced while stationed in North Africa. He kept his mustache waxed and exuded an air of mystery like the bald figure in some of Dali's paintings. After the war, he distinguished himself in the field of electron microscopy by inventing a camera with a millionth-second shutter speed. His den featured a framed photograph of a bullet captured in mid-flight, and another of a large yellow crystal which he titled "The Passing"—his kidney stone a consequence of months in the Libyan desert. There were shaggy trophies on the wall, and startlingly, a mummified elephant's foot serving as an end table next to a stuffed chair. I remember a zebra hide and a Persian rug. His den looked like a disheveled Victorian parlor.

His wife showed us around the premises, proudly displaying the full-length drapes in the living, dining, and master bedrooms which she'd had custom-dyed a subtle shade of chartreuse. Dad and I took note of this because we would be spraying the exterior of the house with solid color stain and didn't want any droplets of oily mist migrating inside. We sealed the windows carefully with plastic. The whole business of spray painting was new to me. Neither Dad nor I used a respirator—we wouldn't have even considered it. The stain contained a toxic brew of toluene and mercury benzene, which I think is illegal now. We blew down the house with that stuff, soaking the thirsty wood with oleaginous Oxford Brown stain. We also did a good job of soaking ourselves. I got so stoned on vapors that at one point I shot my gun straight up at the sky and tried to spray it brown. Then in a stupor I sat on the front steps of the house and tried to figure out how to button my shirt and tie my shoes.

When the paint job was done, we pulled the plastic off the windows and admired our handiwork. We had clambered all over that house like monkeys, infatuated with our wondrous new spray machine. The house practically glowed. Success—or nearly: the owner's wife began noticing little specks of brown inside the house on her exquisite drapes. Everywhere she looked she found more. What on earth was going on? How could our stain have penetrated those windows? We could see our profits swirling down the drain. We went home sick with worry at the end of the day. She immediately had the drapes analyzed by a local laboratory, and they informed her soon enough that the mysterious brown specks were only spider poop.

Dorene and I drove to Boulder last weekend to see the aftermath of the fire and find out if the old shack was still standing. Boulder Canyon was unscathed, but the hills to the north had been ravaged. Our shack was nowhere to be seen. In its place stood an upscale new home, a code-compliant replica of the ramshackle original, with weathertight barnwood siding, a tastefully rusted metal roof, garden with bird feeders gracing the front, and kayak docked in the driveway. Other charming homes had sprung up nearby. Dorene and I sat on a guardrail overlooking the new house, reminiscing about our destitute life there forty years ago. Our fourth child had been conceived there. By the time she was born we had moved to the Crystal River Valley in western Colorado. We had named her Bethany, meaning "house of dates," because we welcomed her arrival as a harbinger of what we hoped would be more prosperous times.

We drove through the fire damage north of Boulder Canyon, where a lot of country got scorched. Everywhere fine ash covered the ground. Black trees stood shell-shocked for ten square miles. The blaze had devoured 166 houses—one of the most destructive fires in Colorado history. Here and there hand-painted signs appeared in front of homes that had been spared. "We love you, firemen! Thank you for your bravery." There was a parade in Boulder on the day we were there, an outpouring of love from a grateful community.

As for the luxury home Dad and I had painted years ago, it still stood as far as I could tell. There were so many fine, new homes scattered along the hogback west of Boulder, I couldn't distinguish one from another. The fire had rampaged up the backside of the hogback, but never made it down to the city.

NOTES

NOTES

49   Paul Petzoldt, 1908-1999, founder of the National Outdoor Leadership School.

52   The author of this motivational poem is unknown.

56   Anthony Greenbank, author of *The Book of Survival*.

64   The Ventures' hit song "Wipeout" stayed on national charts for 4 months in 1963.

64   Barry Goldwater, 1909-1998, ran for President on the Republican ticket in 1964 against incumbent President Lyndon Johnson. He is credited with reinvigorating the conservative movement in the 1960s.

71   Erich Fromm, 1900-1980, a social theorist and philosopher who taught that man should embrace freedom instead of seeking to escape from it.

76   Gaston Rebuffat, 1921-1985, made aesthetic mountaineering films and wrote poetically about the climbing experience.

85   I was particularly influenced toward this view by Alan Watt's *The Book: On the Taboo Against Knowing Who You Are*, based on Hindu philosophy.

89   Hair City, a 5.9 route on the Bastille, Eldorado Canyon State Park, Colorado.

92   Harald Bredesen, 1918-2006, a Lutheran pastor who influenced the lives of Pat Boone, Pat Robertson, and Anwar Sadat. A key figure in the Charismatic Renewal.

105   Reverend Dave Wilkerson founded the first Teen Challenge to help teenage drug addicts and gang members in New York.

110   Topeka State Hospital had a reputation for neglect and abuse, attributable in part to inadequate funding and training. Christianity was viewed by some psychiatrists at that time as an obsessional neurosis.

119   Snowmass Coal, formerly Anschutz Coal, operated mines in the vicinity of North Thompson Creek, southwest of Carbondale. Snowmass installed the first steep-pitching longwall in the U.S. It shut down permanently in 1986.

119-123   Mining terms: The "face" is the freshly exposed seam where coal is being extracted. The "wash plant" is the surface facility where coking coal is separated from useless material such as shale and sandstone. The coal is pulverized, washed, and dried before being loaded onto trucks. "Slopes" are steeply pitching tunnels. The "knuckle," in the way we used the term (probably not proper railroad terminology), was the place where the track began descending at a steep angle. A "caplight" clipped to the hard hat was attached by cable to a rechargeable battery carried on the belt. The "bullgang" is the all-purpose roving work crew. The "fireboss" is a company-employed safety inspector. "Stoppings" are walls erected to direct the course of airflow in the mine. "Ribs" at Snowmass Coal were 8-10 foot vertical walls of virgin coal lining the tunnels.

124   "Bottom heave" occurred because of tectonic forces pushing upward on the rock strata. Sometimes the bottom would push up so forcefully that a tunnel would be squeezed shut. Support timbers would be smashed like toothpicks.

128   The Flattops Wilderness is Colorado's second-largest wilderness area, containing over 300 square miles of subalpine meadows and forests. Astoundingly open country.

150   The Mid-Continent mining operation at Coal Basin, west of Redstone, Colorado, opened in the early 1950s and shut down in 1991. Popularly known as "Mother Mid." It employed 600 workers at its peak.

158 S. Robert Lichter and Stanley Rothman published "Media and Business Elites" in *Public Opinion* in 1981. It was widely discussed in the 1980s and is still regarded as a landmark study.

162 In 1984 the Soviet government sentenced Christian musicians Valeri Barinov and Sergei Timokhin to 2 ½ years of hard labor. Their rock opera, *The Trumpet Call,* was smuggled out of the country and performed in Europe in 1985.

165 Pyotr Rumachik, 1931–, Baptist activist and prisoner of conscience in the Soviet Union.

171 Town of Marble, located in the West Elk mountains of Colorado. Site of the Yule Quarry, from which was extracted the beautiful snow-white marble used in the Tomb of the Unknown Soldier and the Lincoln Memorial. It had a population of about a hundred people in the year 2000.

179 The Roaring Fork Valley community suffered a devastating loss when 15 men were killed in an explosion at Dutch Creek #1 on April 15, 1981. The explosion occurred when an electric spark ignited a pocket of methane gas.

198 *The Divine Revelation of Hell,* by Mary K. Baxter. Not recommended, unless you read Romans and Ephesians along with it. Salvation is by grace.

198 See Dostoevsky's *Notes From Underground*, Part 1, Chapter 2. "The more conscious I became of goodness . . . the more deeply did I sink into the mire . . ."

205 Francis Schaeffer, 1912-1984, Christian theologian, philosopher, and influential figure among Christian conservatives. Author of *Escape From Reason*, among other works.

209 Dad was a fan of Merlin Enabnit, 1903-1979, who propounded the theory of "color surprise" in his how-to painting books.

217   Contra dancing is an old-fashioned form of folk dancing that has made a comeback in recent years. It's usually fairly easy to follow and doesn't require fancy footwork. Way too fun!

219-20   Written in response to "Dream Children; A Reverie," by Charles Lamb.

ART CREDITS

Cover design by George Foster.

Book design by Bobbie Van Meter.

Photographs on pages 172 and 177 by Doug Stewart.

Painting on page 214 by Karen Mata.

All other artwork by the author.

Made in the USA
Lexington, KY
18 July 2014